EVERY
WORD IS A BIRD
WE
TEACH TO SING

ALSO BY DANIEL TAMMET

Born on a Blue Day

Embracing the Wide Sky

Thinking in Numbers

EVERY WORD IS A BIRD WE TEACH TO SING

Encounters with the Mysteries and Meanings of Language

DANIEL TAMMET

Little, Brown and Company

New York   Boston   London

Little, Brown and Company
Hachette Book Group
1290 Avenue of the Americas, New York, NY 10104
littlebrown.com

First Edition: September 2017

Little, Brown and Company is a division of Hachette Book Group, Inc.
The Little, Brown name and logo are trademarks of Hachette Book Group, Inc.

The publisher is not responsible for websites (or their content) that are not owned by the publisher.

The Hachette Speakers Bureau provides a wide range of authors for speaking events. To find out more, go to hachettespeakersbureau.com or call (866) 376-6591.

ISBN 978-0-316-35305-2
LCCN 2017935940

10 9 8 7 6 5 4 3 2 1

LSC-C

Printed in the United States of America

In loving memory of my father

CONTENTS

EVERY
WORD IS A BIRD
WE
TEACH TO SING

One

FINDING MY VOICE

Though English was the language of my parents, the language in which I was raised and schooled, I have never felt I belonged to it. I learned my mother tongue self-consciously, quite often confusedly, as if my mother were a foreigner to me, and her sole language my second. Always, in some corner of my child mind, a running translation was struggling to keep up. To say this word or that word in other words. To recompose the words of a sentence like so many pieces of a jigsaw puzzle. Years before doctors informed me of my high-functioning autism and the disconnect it causes between man and language, I had to figure out the world as best I could. I was a misfit. The world was made up of words. But I thought and felt and sometimes dreamed in a private language of numbers.

In my mind each number had a shape—complete with color and texture and occasionally motion (a neurological phenomenon that scientists call synesthesia)—and each shape a meaning. The meaning could be pictographic: eighty-nine, for instance, was dark blue, the color of a sky threatening storm; a beaded texture; and a fluttering, whirling, downward motion I understood as "snow" or, more broadly, "winter." I remember, one winter, seeing snow fall outside my bedroom window for the first time. I was seven. The snow, pure white and thick-flaked, piled many inches high upon the ground, transforming the gray concrete of the neighborhood into a virgin, opalescent tundra. "Snow," I gasped to my parents. "Eighty-nine," I thought. The thought had hardly crossed my mind when I had another: nine hundred and seventy-nine. The view from my window resembled nine hundred and seventy-nine—the shimmer and beauty of eleven expanding, literally multiplying eighty-nine's wintry swirl. I felt moved. My parents' firstborn, I had been delivered at the end of a particularly cold and snowy January in 1979. The coincidence did not escape me. Everywhere I looked, it seemed, there were private meanings writ large.

Was it from that moment—the sudden sense that my meanings corresponded to the wider world—that I first had the urge to communicate? Until that moment, I had never felt the need to open up to another person: not to my parents or siblings, let alone to any of the other children at my school. Now, suddenly, a feeling lived in me, for which I had neither name nor number (it was a little like the sadness of six, but different). I eventually learned the feeling was what we call loneliness. I had no friends. But how could I make myself understood to children from whom I felt so estranged? We spoke differently, thought differently. The other children hadn't the faintest idea (how could they?) that the relationship between eighty-nine and nine hundred and seventy-nine was like the relationship between, say, *diamond* and *adamant*. And with what words might I have explained that eleven and forty-nine, my mental logograms, rhymed? A visual rhyme. I would have liked nothing better than to share with my classmates some of my poems made of numbers:

Sixty-one two two two two eleven
One hundred and thirty-one forty-nine

But I kept the poems to myself. The children at school intimidated me. In the playground every mouth was a shout, a snort, an insult. And the more the children roared, the more they laughed and joked in my direction, the less I dared approach them and attempt to strike up a conversation. Besides, I did not know what a conversation sounded like.

I renounced the idea of making friends. I had to admit that I wasn't ready. I retreated into myself, into the certainties of my numerical language. Alone with my thoughts in the relative calm and quiet of my bedroom, I dwelled on my number shapes, on their grammar. One hundred and eighty-one, a prime number, was a tall shiny symmetrical shape like a spoon. When I doubled it—modified its shape with that of two, which was a sort of "doing" number—it equated to a verb. So that three hundred and sixty-two had the meaning of "to eat" or "to consume" (more literally, "to move a spoon"). It was the mental picture that always announced that I was hungry. Other pictures that rose up in me could morph in a similar way, depending on the action they described and whether it was external or internal to me: thirteen (a rhythmic descending motion) if a raindrop on the windowpane caught my gaze, twenty-six if I tired and sensed myself drifting off to sleep.

My understanding of language as something visual carried

over to my relationship with books once I became a library-goer and regularly tugged large, slender, brightly colored covers down from the shelves. Even before I could make out the words, I fell under the spell of *The Adventures of Tintin*. The boy with the blond quiff and his little sidekick dog, Snowy. Speech in bubbles; emotions in bold characters and exclamation marks; the story smoothly unfolding from picture to altered picture. Each frame was fit to pore over, so finely and minutely detailed: a mini-story in itself. Stories within stories, like numbers within numbers: I was mesmerized.

The same understanding, the same excitement, also helped me learn to read. This was my luck, since reading had not initially come easily to me. Except for the occasional word of comfort the night after a nightmare, my parents never read me bedtime stories, and because the antiepileptic medicine I was prescribed at a young age made me drowsy in class, I was never precocious. I have memories of constantly falling pages behind the other children, of intense bouts of concentration in order to catch up. My delight in the shapes of the words in my schoolbooks, their visual impression on me, made the difference. One of the books, I remember, contained an illustration of a black-cloaked witch, all sharp angles, astride her broom. To my six-year-old imagination, the letter *W* was a pair of witches' hats, side by side and hanging upside down, as from a nail.

Back in those days, the mid-eighties, it was possible for a teacher to give her young charge a repurposed tobacco tin (mine was dark-green and gold) in which new words, written in clear letters on small rectangular cards, were to be brought home for learning. From that time on I kept a list of words according to their shape and texture: words round as a three (*gobble, cupboard, cabbage*); pointy as a four (*jacket, wife, quick*); shimmering as a five (*kingdom, shoemaker, surrounded*). One day, intent on my reading, I happened on *lollipop* and a shock of joy coursed through me. I read it as *1011ipop*. One thousand and eleven, divisible by three, was a fittingly round number shape, and I thought it the most beautiful thing I had yet read: half number and half word.

I grew; my vocabulary grew. Curt sentences in my schoolbooks' prim typeset; lessons the teacher chalked up on the blackboard; breathless adjectives on crinkly flyers that intruded via the letterbox; pixelated headlines in the pages of Ceefax ("See Facts"), the BBC's teletext service. All these and many more besides I could read and write, and spell backward as well as forward, but not always pronounce. Only rarely did words reach me airborne, via a radio or a stranger's mouth. (I watched television for the pictures—I was forever lowering the sound.) If I surprised my father talking to the milkman at the door, or my mother sharing gossip with a neighbor over the garden fence, I would try to listen in—and abruptly tune out. As sounds and social currency, words could not yet hold me. Instead, I lavished my attention on arranging and rearranging them into sentences, playing with them as I played with the number shapes in my head, measuring the visual effect of, for instance, interlacing round three-y words with pointy four-y ones, or of placing several five-y words, all agleam, in a row.

A classmate called Babak was the first person to whom I showed my sentences. He was his parents' image. They were thin, gentle people who had fled the Ayatollah's Iran several years before for the anonymity of a London suburb; they had recently enrolled their son at my school. Babak was reassuringly unlike the other children, with his thick black hair and crisp English and a head both for words and numbers. In his backyard one warm weekend, sitting opposite me on the grass, he looked up from the Scrabble board to read the crumpled sheet of lined notepaper I was nervously holding out to him.

"Interesting. Is it a poem?"

I sat still, my head down, staring at a spot between the numbered tiles. I could feel his inquisitive brown eyes on me. Finally, I shrugged and said, "I don't know."

"Doesn't matter. It's interesting."

This was also the opinion of my headmaster. How exactly my writing reached him remains, to this day, something of a mystery to me. I was ten. The class had been reading H. G. Wells's *The War of the Worlds*; and, in a state of high excitement induced by the graphic prose, I had been rushing home every day after class to the solitude of my bedroom to write— cautiously, to begin with, then compulsively. Of this story, my first sustained piece of writing, my mind has retained only fragments: winding descriptions of labyrinthine tunnels; outlines of sleek spaceships that blot out the sky; laser guns spending laser bullets, turning the air electric. No dialogue. The story inhabited me, overpowered me. It quickly exceeded every line of every page of every pad of notepaper in the house. So that the first my teacher heard of it was the afternoon, after class, when I blushed crimson and asked whether I might help myself to a roll of the school's computer printout paper. I could, but in exchange I had to confide in her the purpose. The following week, softly, she asked me how the story was coming along. She wanted to see it. I went away and brought back, with difficulty, the many pages filled with my tiny, neat hand to her desk. She said to leave them with her. I hesitated, then agreed. Did she, upon reading the story, decide to urge it upon the headmaster? Or did the headmaster, visiting the teacher or simply passing by, happen on it? However it came to him, one morning during the school assembly, breaking from his usual headmaster patter, he announced that he was going to read an extract from my story to the hall. I hadn't expected that. Not without so much as a word of warning from my teacher! I had never seen the headmaster read aloud a pupil's work. I couldn't bring myself to listen along with the other students. Out of nerves and embarrassment, I put my palms to my ears—it was one of my habits—and fixed my eyes on the whorls of dust on the floor. But after the assembly, children who had never so much as given me the time of day came up and greeted me smilingly, tapping me on the shoulders, saying "Great story" or words to that effect. The headmaster would have awarded my story a prize, he made a point of telling me later in his office, if only he had had such a prize to give. His encouragement was a fine enough substitute, which I treasured. So I was crestfallen when I had to move on to high school soon afterward and, in lieu of deploying my imagination to compose new stories, was made to regurgitate umpteen examination-friendly facts. The talent peeping out from under my shyness and social bewilderment I would have to nourish more or less on my own, I realized, foraging for whatever extracurricular sustenance I might find.

It was among the bookcases of the municipal library that

I spent most of my adolescence, as fluent by then in the deciphering of texts as I remained inept in conversation. These years of reading, I see now, were a way of apprenticing myself with voices of wisdom, the multitudinous accents of human experience, listening sedulously to each with my bespectacled eyes. Growing in empathy book by book, from puberty onward I increasingly set aside the illustrated encyclopedias and dictionaries in favor of history books, biographies, and memoirs. I pushed myself to go further still, intellectually and emotionally, into the fatter novels of Adult Fiction.

I was afraid of this kind of fiction. Afraid of feeling lost in the intricacies of a social language I had not mastered (and feared I never might). Afraid that the experience would shake whatever small self-confidence I had. A good part of the fault for this lay on my high school English classes and their "required reading." If Shakespeare — his outlandish characters and strange diction (which we read in a side-by-side translation to contemporary English) — had fascinated me, Dickens had seemed interminable and Hardy's *Jude the Obscure* very obscure indeed.

But in the municipal library I had the freedom of the shelves. I could browse at my ease. The works I looked at were not the thematic or didactic stories told by wordy, know-it-all narrators that examiners use for their set questions. They were shorter novels by living writers: artfully concise personal reflections on modern life (ranging from the 1950s to the year just past) written by and for a socioeconomic class that was not my own. But for all that, they were approachable. Partly I went to them for the past readers' marginalia — for the crabbed, scribbled words of agreement or annoyance or wonder, which imparted unintended clues to the meaning of a particular sentence or paragraph. Also for the creases and thumbprints and coffee stains on the pages, reminders that books are also social objects—gateways between our internal and external worlds. And partly for the characters' dialogue, their verbal back-and-forth clearly set out and punctuated, integral to the story. So this is how people talk, I would think, as I read. This is what conversation looks like.

And some nights, I dreamed I watched the dialogic patterns converted into my number shapes:

"Twelve seventy one nine two hundred and fifty-seven."

"Two hundred and fifty-seven?"

"Two!"

"Four. Sixteen."

"Seventeen."

When I was nearing matriculation from high school, Frau Corkhill, who had been my German teacher for several years, began inviting me over to her house for late-afternoon lessons in conversation—more in English than German.

I sorely needed such practice. Outside of the family, where so much can be meant and understood without even needing to utter a word, I was able to say little that didn't come out sounding clunky, off-topic, or plain odd. For templates I relied mostly on the dialogues I had studied in the library novels; but such schemas, however many I studied, however well performed, would only ever, I came to realize, get me so far. I was almost a young man: the urge to communicate had begun to take on a new charge. One day, in history class, the sight of a new boy brought my thumping heart into my throat, and my attraction compelled me to try to converse with him. I talked and talked, happy to be anxious, but what had looked so good and persuasive on the page of a novel fell flat in my strangled voice, which was unpracticed and monotonous. The courage I'd mustered vanished into mortification. More than mortification. Seven hundred and fifty-seven (a shape which I can only compare to a ginger root): an acute feeling — arising from immense desire to communicate, aligned with a commensurate incapacity to do so — for which English has no precise equivalent.

Frau Corkhill was a short and stout and red-haired woman, at retirement age or thereabouts, and the object of much sniggering from some of the pupil population for her various eccentricities. She ate raw garlic cloves by the bulbful. She wore flower print dresses and fluorescent socks. She merely smiled a bright red lipstick smile and gazed up wistfully at the ceiling when any other teacher would have bawled an undisciplined student out of the room. Such behavior was, in my view, neither here nor there. She doted on me. She was like a grandmother to me. She seemed to intuit the invisible difficulties against which I had fought all through my childhood. I remember the day she gave me her telephone number, an attractive medley of fours and sevens, shortly before I was to change classes. The first three digits after the area code became my nickname for her. Before long, I called and accepted her invitation to the house. Every week for the next year, I rode the red double-decker the twenty or so minutes to her door.

These lessons-slash-discussions with Frau Corkhill were

the highlight of my week. She was a woman of infinite patience, a professional at making light of others' mistakes, at correcting by example rather than by admonishment. Her home was a space in which I could talk and exchange without fear of being taken for a conversational klutz. We sat in the living room next to a bay window overlooking the rose garden, on high-backed chairs at a table dressed in a frilly white cloth, a tray and china tea set in its center, like a scene out of a library novel.

We talked about the school, about whatever was in the news. Sometimes we changed language, English to German and back again. Frau Corkhill's English was unique, her accent part German and part Geordie (*Corkhill,* her married name, is a common surname in northern England). Strange to think, I had not noticed people's accents before. Strange to remember my surprise when a classmate informed me that my pronunciation of *th* was off (my Cockney father's fault). I had not known to notice.

But now, talking with Frau Corkhill, I understood how many Englishes must exist. Hers, mine: two among countless others.

In writing the story of my formative years in the words I had back in 2005 (I was twenty-six), with feeling but without confidence or high finish, I found my voice. The international success of *Born on a Blue Day* began a conversation with readers from around the world. Where some British and American critics saw only a one-off "disability genre" memoir, the account of a "numbers wiz," German and Spanish and Brazilian and Japanese readers saw something else, and sent letters urging me to continue writing. Many referred to a closing chapter in which I recounted a public reading I had given at the Museum of the History of Science, in Oxford, in 2004. The subject of my reading was not a book, not the work of any published name, but a number: pi. Over the three preceding wintry months, like an actor analyzing his script, I had rehearsed the number from home, assimilating its unstinting digits by the hundreds of hundreds, until I knew the first 22,514, a European record's worth, by heart. On the fourteenth of March, I narrated this most beautiful of epic poems, an *Odyssey* or an *Iliad* composed of numbers, in a performance spanning five hours, to the hall. For the first time in my life I spoke aloud in my numerical language (albeit, necessarily, in English words), at length, passionately, fluently. And if, in the early minutes of my recitation, I worried that the small crowd of curious listeners might comprehend about as much as if I were performing in Chinese, shake their heads, turn their backs on me and leave, all my fears quickly evaporated. As I gathered momentum, acquired rhythm, I sensed the men and women lean forward, alert and rapt. With each pronounced digit their concentration redoubled and silenced competing thoughts. Meditative smiles broadened faces. Some in the audience were even moved to tears. In those numbers I had found the words to express my deepest emotions. In my person, through my breath and body, the numbers spoke to the motley attendees on that bright March morning and afternoon.

The numbers also spoke through the printed page to my far-flung readers, came alive in their minds, regardless of the translation that conveyed them. My lifelong struggle to find my voice, my obsession with language, appeared to them, as it did to me, like a vocation.

I'd written a book and had it published. But it remained unclear whether a young man on the autistic spectrum could have other books in him. No tradition of autistic writing existed (indeed, some thought *autistic author* a contradiction in terms). I had no models (though, later, I made the discovery that Lewis Carroll—possibly—and Les Murray, the Australian poet and Nobel Prize candidate, to name only two, shared my condition), no material. I was on my own.

But then another reader's letter arrived. It was in French, a language I had studied in high school, from a young Frenchman named Jérôme, who would, in time, become my husband. Through months of thoughtful and playful correspondence, Jérôme and I fell in love. For him, for his country and language, I chose willingly to leave the country and the language I had never felt were mine. We moved to Avignon, then north to Paris, settling among the bistros and *bouquinistes* of Saint-Germain-des-Prés.

Before Jérôme, I had largely given up on literature. Novels and I had long since parted company. Now, though, in our apartment, surrounded by our books (Jérôme owned many books), we sat together at a brown teak table and, taking turns, read aloud from the French translation of Dostoyevsky's *L'Idiot*. My voice when I read, as when I had recited the number pi, seemed at once intimate and distant: another voice in mine, enlarging and enriching it. And, as with pi, I understood and became enthralled.

Reading a Russian work in French, I was not invaded by

the feeling of foreignness that the pages of English novels had roused in me. On the contrary, I felt at home. I could, at last, read unencumbered by my self-consciousness, solely for the pleasure of learning new words and discovering new worlds. I could read for the sake of reading.

Dostoyevsky's reputation, a powerful intermediary between his work and modern readers, would once have daunted and kept me away. But Dostoyevsky's language proved to be picture perfect. A case in point is the character General Ivolgin, the smell of whose cigar provokes a haughty English lady traveling with her lapdog in the same compartment to pluck the cigar from between his fingers and toss it out the train. Yet the general just sits there, seemingly unfazed by the lady's behavior. Quick as a flash and ever so smoothly, he leans over and chucks her little dog out after his cigar. I remember my voice, in the telling, interrupted by my own shocked laughter, and how my merriment communicated itself to Jérôme and had him in stitches.

It wasn't only Dostoyevsky who could so affect us. In the following months we laughed and gasped over Isaac Babel's short stories. Kawabata's *Le Grondement de la Montagne* (*The Sound of the Mountain*) — the tale of an old man's ailing memory — brought tears to my voice. The visual music of *Paroles* by Jacques Prévert reverberated in my head long after I closed its covers.

Then, one day, as if removing the stabilizers from a child's bicycle, Jérôme ceased to accompany my literary reading. I did not wobble. And, after devouring both tomes of Tolstoy's *Guerre et Paix,* I tried the Russian master's *Anna Karenina* in English, and the heroine's passions, Levin's and

Kitty's foibles, Vronsky's contradictions all affected me so greatly that I clean forgot the apprehension of my former reading life. Something had worked itself in my head. All literature, I finally realized with a jolt, amounted to an act of translation: a condensing, a sifting, a realignment of the author's thought-world into words. The reassuring corollary — reassuring to a novice writer like myself, just starting out: the translatorese of bad prose could be avoided, provided the words were faithful to the mental pictures the author saw. I had more than one book in me. And each of my subsequent books — a survey of popular neuroscience, a collection of essays inspired by mathematical ideas, a translation/adaptation into French of Les Murray's poetry — was different. Each taught me what my limits weren't. I could do this. And this. And this as well. All the time that I was writing, I was also studying in my after-hours with the UK's distance learning higher education institution, the Open University. In 2016, at the age of thirty-seven, I graduated with a first-class honors bachelor of arts degree in the humanities. I published my first novel that same spring in France.

I have not yet written my last English sentence, despite ten years spent on the continent and despite the increasing distillation of my words from French. That choice, renewed here, is an homage to my British parents and teachers. A recognition, too, of the debt I owe to a language commodious enough even for a voice like mine. English made a foreigner of me, but also a writer. It has become the faithful chronicler of my metamorphosis.

Two

THE LANGUAGE TEACHER

Everything I know about teaching a foreign language, I learned in Lithuania.

It was 1998. I was nineteen, unready for university, full of wanderlust and good intentions. I enrolled in a government-run volunteer program that sent young men and women overseas. I could have been sent to Poland to nanny little Mateuszes and Weronikas or to a clinic in Russia short of file finders or to wash dishes in a hotel who knows where in the Czech Republic or to the British embassy in Slovenia, whose front desk needed manning.

Instead I was dispatched to Lithuania, to the city of Kaunas. I couldn't speak a word of Lithuanian. My innocence of the language didn't seem to matter, though. A young Englishman with passable French and German (Lithuanian bore no relation to either) was apparently sufficient for instructing the job-seeking inhabitants eager to learn English.

I remember taking the airplane from London to the capital city of Vilnius. The thrill of takeoff. To feel airborne! No one in my family had ever flown before. "Head in the clouds," my father had sometimes said of me. And now his words, once a mere expression, had come literally true.

The nations of the former Soviet Union were shown to us in Western newscasts as uniformly gray, dilapidated, Russified. But the Lithuania I arrived in, only a few years after Moscow's tanks had slunk away, had reason for optimism. The population was youngish, new shiny buildings were sprouting up here and there, and, despite fifty years of foreign occupation, Lithuanian habits and customs had lived on.

It took time to adjust. Little shocks of unfamiliarity had to be absorbed. October in London was autumnal; in Kaunas, the cold reminded me of a British winter. Snow was already in the offing. And then there was the funny money, the *litas,* in which my volunteer stipends were paid. But strangest, in those first days, was the language, so unlike the sounds and rhythms of any other language I had heard. An old man in my apartment block stops me in the stairwell to tell me something keen and musical — what is it? Children in the street sing a song — what is it about? Unintelligible, too, were the headlines and captions the inky newspapers carried. They looked like a secret code. How I wished to work out the cipher!

A code breaker. But the Lithuanian learning kit the program's staff had given me was small. In less experienced hands, the kit — really a pocket dictionary and phrasebook — would have seemed futile; there was nothing an imagination could fasten onto. I knew better. I sat at my apartment desk, opened the dictionary, about the size of a deck of cards, and flicked the wispy, nearly transparent pages to the word for *language: kalba.* As words went, it struck me as beautiful. Beautiful and fitting. Suddenly other words, in other languages, swam in my head: the English *gulp,* the Finnish *kello* ("bell"). Less the words than the various meanings behind them: *gulp,* a mouthful of air; *bell,* a metal tongue. In this way, *kalba* I understood intuitively as something of the mouth, of the tongue. (Like *language,* whose Latin ancestor, *lingua,* means "tongue.")

Fingering the pages again, hearing them crinkle, I turned them at random and read *puodelis,* cup. If *kalba* was a word to savor, *puodelis,* I felt, belonged between the palms. I closed my eyes and rubbed my hands together as though palping the syllables: *puo-de-lis, puo-de-lis.*

I roved five pages, ten, as many as I could soak up in a sitting. My eyes went from entry to entry. I was looking for the kind of wonderful juxtaposition you otherwise see in the fairy tale and the surrealist poem, the kind at which the unwitting lexicographer excels. *Cat hair* and *cathedral. Mushroom* and *music-hall. Umbrella* and *umbilical* cord. Lithuanian, in this respect, can be just as Grimm or Dada, let me tell you. A short way into the *D's,* I hit on the Lithuanian for *thistle* and *combustible* — in the words of my dictionary, *dagis* and *dagus* — two ordinarily distinct ideas only a vowel apart. They recalled Exodus, put a Baltic twist on the story of Moses and the burning bush. Musing over this, I could not help asking myself, what sermon would a desert thistle have spoken?

What surprises this pungent little dictionary contained! What pleasure! And the more pages I turned, the more my pleasure in its company grew. In the excitement and anxiety of those first days in Kaunas we became inseparable.

A week after my arrival I was already on the job, teaching for two hours Monday through Friday at a women's center in the city's downtown, a trolleybus ride away from my apartment. In the classroom, the dozen women in front of me didn't look at all like the squat, kerchiefed babushkas I scrimmaged with each morning on the bus. They wore smart skirts and makeup and their hair in varying degrees of stylishness. And when, during our first lesson, I introduced myself and tried out some words of Lithuanian, they chuckled good-naturedly at my accent—the women had never heard their language in a British voice before. I asked them their reasons for coming. One student, Birutė (a common name, I learned), turned into something of a spokeswoman for the others. She stood up and said, in excellent English, "We want to improve our English. Because English has become the language of skilled employment here. If you speak Lithuanian and Russian and Polish but no English, you are worse than illiterate. Look at the job advertisements in the newspapers! *Anglų kalba reikalinga*, 'English required.'"

Birutė was by far the strongest student. She was in her forties, very slim and elegant, her dyed black hair cut boyishly short. "I studied English at university. But that was long ago." Her confidence in her English sometimes wavered.

Aida, Birutė's friend, wanted to say something as well. She was younger than Birutė, and shyer. Her voice was soft and hesitant. Understandably so. All she had for English were a few scattered phrases. Birutė intervened. "She says

21

she hopes you will do better than the last teacher. An American. She says she could not follow a word he said."

At Aida's comments the other women in the class began shouting all at the same time, apparently eager to join in the criticism of my predecessor. Their shouts held months of accumulated frustration, annoyance, despair. Down with boring textbooks! Down with pedagogic jargon! We want to learn English, not a bunch of useless rules!

I was taken aback. I had expected the calm of a classroom; I hadn't expected this brouhaha. To tell the truth, I started to feel a bit afraid. And I was embarrassed by my fear. I thought, I'm nineteen. I don't know what to tell them. I've only just arrived here. I was of two minds whether or not to walk out.

Just then Birutė waved her arms and hollered something at the room. An awkward silence came over the women.

"*Atsiprašau* ['excuse me']," she said. "I should not [have] let Aida say what she said. She becomes excited and excites the others. We are very happy and we thank you for teaching us your language."

We spent the rest of our first encounter looking at the textbooks provided by the center and trying to get some sort of discussion going. But the women were right. The pages were soporific beyond any teacher's skill or enthusiasm. If I continued to work from them, as the volunteer before me had, whatever remained of the women's hopes of speaking serviceable English might have been crushed for good. I resolved to drop the book. To teach differently. How? I did not know. Even so, my attitude was that I would find another approach in time for the next lesson.

I racked my brain to find a more natural, more enjoyable, method.

It came to me late that evening at my apartment while I sat in an armchair reading from the little Lithuanian-English dictionary as had become my habit. I was up to the letter O when the entry *obuolys* ("apple") made me stop and put the book down. I closed my eyes. Suddenly I recalled the moment, ten years ago, when I discovered the existence of non-English words, that is to say, other nations' languages.

Back in east London, exceedingly shy, almost house-bound, I had gotten to know one of my kid sister's girl-friends, who lived a few doors down. The blond mother of this blond girl was Finnish (I had no idea what *Finnish* meant), and, to teach her daughter the language, one day she gave her a bright Finnish picture book. The gift, as it turned out, went unopened; the girl had no interest in words my sister and her other friends would never have under-stood. She left the picture book with us.

Cover-wise it looked like any other unthumbed picture book, but once inside I sat astonished. On every page, below the colorful illustration of an everyday object, a word that didn't quite look like a word. A word intended for another kind of child. Finnish!

Of all the impressions this book made on me, the red apple accompanied by the noun *omena* left the deepest. There was something about the distribution of the vowels, the roundness of the consonants, that fascinated. I felt that I was seeing double, for the picture seemed to mirror the word and vice versa. Both word and picture represented an apple by means of lines.

The next day, on my way to the center, I stopped in at a grocery store and bought a bag of apples. When the women filed into the classroom and saw the pyramid of red and green apples on my table, I said, "Yesterday some of you said you knew no English. That's not true. You know lots of English words. You know *bar*."

"*Baras*," Aida said.

"Right. And *restaurant*."

One of the women at the back shouted, "*Restoranas*."

"Yes. And *history, istorija*, and *philosophy, filosofija*."

Birutė, sitting near the front, said, "*Telephone*."

"*Telefonas*. You see? Lots of words." I turned to the apples.

"*Taksi*," someone said.

"Yes, well, the list is long. What about these on my table?"

The women replied as one, "*Obuoliai!*"

Apples.

I told my students about the picture book, and the story of the red apple. Birutė translated for me. I said, "If you can draw an apple, you can learn the word *apple*." After I had asked them to take out their pencils and paper, I went to lift and give out the pile of fruit; but I misjudged the gesture and heard the hapless apples slip from my grasp and roll off along the floor.

Women's laughter.

I bent down and picked up the apples and put one on each of the student's desks. I was laughing, too. But concentration quickly replaced the levity. Heads were lowered; brows were creased; pencils were plied. A quarter of an hour or so later I told the students to stop. Their drawings ranged from colored-in circles to Birutė's delicate sketch, complete with shading.

"When you put pencil to paper you don't draw the apple as such, you draw its shape and texture and color," Birutė translated. "Each aspect is proportional to the drawer's experiences. So one apple might be round like a tennis ball; a second, glossy as plastic; a third, baby-cheek red." I said the word *apple* was another form of drawing. "You draw *a-p-p-l-e*." As I spoke, I wrote the letters in red on the whiteboard. "An initial *A,* consecutive *P*'s, an *L,* and a final *E.* Your imagination can play with them as it plays with shape and color. Mix them around. Subtract or add a letter. Tweak the sound of *P* to *B*." In the way that an apple can make a sketcher think of a tennis ball, or plastic, or a baby's cheeks, an *apple* can bring to an English mind a *stable,* or a *cobbler,* or *pulp,* I explained.

Then I told the women to take out their dictionaries and find other *apple*-like words.

Birutė's face lit up: she understood. Her pen, busy with words, ran quickly across the sheet of paper. The others wrote more tentatively. Empty lines glared at the women with least English.

"Turn the pages of your dictionary in the direction of the

letter *P*," I encouraged. "Look for possible words in combinations like *P* something *L,* or *PL* something, or *P* something
something *L,* and so on. Or turn to the front and search for
words that begin *BL.* Or think about how English words
handle a pair of *P*'s or *B*'s, how they push them to the
middle — *apple* and *cobble* — or out to the extremes — *pulp.*
Birutė, can you translate that please?" Birutė repeated my
words, but in Lithuanian.

When the students had finished writing down their findings, they took turns reading them aloud to the class. One
lady came up with *bulb;* another, *appetite;* a third, *palpable.*
A fourth in the corner, relishing the sudden attention of the
room, shouted, "Plop!" Just the sound conjured apples falling out of trees from ripeness.

"Apple pie," Aida suggested suddenly.

I nodded. On the whiteboard appeared *apple pie.*

Out of her store of words, duly put to paper, Birutė joined
in: "Pips. Peel. Plate. Ate. Eat."

I was delighted. She had let the language think for her.

We stayed with the exercise for the following lessons. We
found *car* in *chair* and *wet* in *towel,* and *window* brought us,
word by word, to *interview;* and as the students' vocabularies
filled out, so did their confidence. The mood in the classroom lightened; betterment seemed only another lesson
away. Even those with the least English found themselves
writing and speaking more and more. Enthusiastic students
don't make good dunces.

Some English words, my students and I decided, are dia-
grams. We looked at *look* — the *o*'s like eyes; and at how the

letters in *dog*—the *d* like a left-looking head, the *g* like a tail—limned the animal. We admired the symmetry, so apt, of *level*. Other words are optical illusions: *moon*, after you have covered the first or third leg of the letter *m,* turns night into day: *noon. Desserts* is a mouth-waterer of a word, or a mouth-dryer, depending on which direction—left to right, or right to left—the reader takes it in. Still other words are like successive images in a flip book. See how the *T* advances:

Stain
Satin
Saint

I spent a whole lesson explaining a type of word I might have classified as impressionistic. They are the words that most sway the eye, tease the ear, intrigue the tongue. Those that give off a certain vibe just by their being seen and heard and repeated. Consider *slant*, I said. I wrote the word on the whiteboard. Did Birutė know it? No, Birutė didn't know it. None of the students had read or heard it before. That could have made them tetchily impatient, but it didn't. With my new teacher's nerves abating, and Birutė translating, I felt sure I wasn't in any danger of losing the room. I was in complete command. So I said, "Let's stay a few moments with *slant*. What kind of a word picture is *slant?* Do its letters, their corresponding sounds, give the impression that the word refers to something light or heavy? Or to something opaque? Shiny? Smooth?" (Part of teaching a language is educating your student's guesses, taming them.) Opinion in the class was divided. A good many of the women, though, said the sight and sound made them think of something negative rather than positive, something on the heavy side. I went to the spot on the board beside *slant* and continued writing: *sleep, slide, slope,* and *slump.* What did they all have in common? Visually, and audibly, lots. The words were the same length; they had the same onset — *sl;* they closed on a *p, t,* or *d.* And their meanings? I raised my left hand to eye level and lowered it. *Sleep:* a stander or sitter lies down. *Slide* and *slope:* a descent. *Slump:* a company's stock plummets. The words formed a polyptych, a series of interrelated pictures. *Slant,* then? The women raised their hands and lowered them. "Like this," I said, raising my left hand again and lowering it diagonally: my hand, a translator of *slant.*

With the forefinger of my left hand I drew a circle around my nose and mouth. *"Smell,"* I said. *"Smile."* I smiled. *"Smirk."* I made a face. *"Smoke."* I brought an air cigarette to my lips. *"Smother."* I clapped a palm over my mouth. *"Sneeze."* I pretended to sneeze. *"Snore."* I pretended to snore. *"Sniff,"* I said, sniffing. *"Sneer,"* I said, sneering. Another polyptych in words.

"Snail," Birutė said. "What about *snail?"*

"Like tongues," I said. "Tongues with shells." And added, once the laughter had subsided, "Of course, not every word fits into a particular frame."

But many did. Our imaginations, during part of the rest of the lesson, painted in *thump*s and *stomp*s and *bump*s and *whomp*s the colors of a bruise. Next, the broken, kinetic lines of z's — like moving points which have lost their way — excited in us a sensation of perplexity: ears *buzzed* as though filled with *jazz,* eyes were *dazzled,* heads felt *fuzzy* and *dizzy.* At the end of class, the other side of *drizzle* and *blizzard,* the women left with their senses thoroughly soaked.

Always I situated the words the students would learn in sentences. Every sentence was an experiment in composition; I was less interested in realistic description. I wanted the women to view the words from different perspectives, to study the effects of layout on meaning, to understand grammar as the arranging and blending of sounds and letters.

"Wind down the window!"

"The secondhand watch's second hand has stopped."

"Her teacher's smooth ink taught thought."

Winter came, Lithuanian style. It snowed and snowed and snowed. (*Snow.* What does it have to do with the mouth or nose? Some memories of my childhood in winter are of tasting snowflakes melt on the tip of my tongue.) Ground-floor homes were up to their windowsills in snow. I shivered, one floor up, in my drafty apartment built before double glazing, on a street that is forgivably forgotten by tourist maps. Under a blanket I curled up with the pocket dictionary and watched the weather on TV. Compared to Britain's and the female forecaster's long trim outlines, Lithuania appeared somewhat bulky and flat. The temperatures in every part of the country were all preceded by minuses. I had never before seen the numbers go so low.

To take my mind off my shivering, I turned to a page near the end of the dictionary. My Lithuanian was coming along. I was finally able to understand the old man's neighborly banter when he stopped me as I carried my groceries up the stairs. The headlines on display at kiosks had become as mundane to me as any in London. And my feel for the language was improving; I noticed myself noticing more and more, making more and more connections — like the entries on this page under the letter *V*. They were loud words, those that began with *var-*. The sounds they depicted were predictable, repetitive. I looked at the words of this polyptych and heard the caw of *varna*, a crow; the ribbet of *varlė*, a frog; the ding-dong of *varpas*, a bell; the chug of *variklis*, an engine; the drone of *vargonai*, an organ; the squeak of *vartai*, a gate. I heard someone shout my *vardas*, my name, over and over again. I listened to the verb *varvėti*, "to drip," its familiar tin drumbeat.

Jo vardas Valdas. ("His name is Valdas.")

Iš variklio varva benzinas. ("Petrol drips from the engine.")

Soon my Lithuanian outgrew the pocket dictionary. I was hungry for other books. But on the shelves in the apartment's living room stood only black-and-white photos: a thin man in a dark suit, a thinner woman in a pale dress. The landlord's family, I presumed. No novels. Zero stories. Years of communism had been hard on language. Schoolbooks singing the praises of Comrades Lenin and Stalin had given the printed word a bad name. I turned the apartment upside down. I pulled out drawers: buttons, discontinued stamps, a sprinkling of rusty coins. I opened the cupboard abutting the bedroom: a bottle of vodka, four-fifths bottle, one-fifth vodka. In the closet, beneath a spare bedspread, I dredged up only a yellowing telephone directory. I thought, if I want to read, I'd better join the city library.

At the library I had to fill out forms. *"Vardas,"* the top of the form asked. I wrote my name and, under it, the apartment's address. I gave the women's center as my employer. The muted man at the desk exchanged my responses for a pass and watched the library's newest recruit set out among the aisles. I roamed from bookcase to bookcase, pausing here and there to sample the pages. Quickly, however, my initial excitement shriveled. So dull, the Soviet-era books, so very dry. So full of the words for work and happiness. Work, work, work. Happiness, happiness, happiness. As the Lithuanians say, thanks for the poppies, but I would like bread. I almost gave up.

But chance intervened. I had wandered out to the dust-collecting reaches of the library. I stumbled on a slim volume—very old to judge by the worn, flaky cover—by a poet named Kazys Binkis. Suddenly my imagination woke up. Clouds that sauntered like calves along fields of sky; forests in May colors; recipes in which thoughts were measured out in grams—I instantly decided not to hand in my pass. "Was there perhaps a bilingual edition?" I asked one of the librarians. I was thinking of using it in my class. The sallow, gray-haired librarian (he didn't look like he had ever tasted a snowflake) shook his head. He pointed at a remote bookcase—foreign literature; *foreign* here meaning English, mostly—where I found an anthology of British and American poems and checked it out with the Binkis. The library's poetry section henceforth kept my students and me in texts.

I was coming out of the classroom one afternoon when I heard the director's door open, heard my name called in her stentorian voice, and her jewelry jingle as she stepped back inside her office. It wasn't the first time that the director had asked a staff member into her office, but until now, if her voice resounded in the center, it was never with the curiously accented syllables of "DAN-i-el." When I tapped at her door and went in, she was at her desk leafing through the English textbook. The impressive perm made her head look very big. She said, "I hear strange things about your class. I don't understand. What a secretary of bees? What does it mean?" My students had steadily been working through the library's anthology, and in the past few lessons we had been looking at the poems of Sylvia Plath. "Here is the secretary of bees" is from "The Bee Meeting," I explained.

"But there no such thing. No such thing as secretary of bees." Incomprehension aged her. She was suddenly all frowns and worry lines. "It not correct English. The center has textbooks to teach correct English. See?" Her ringed finger tapped a sentence on the page in front of her. "Here. Like this." She read aloud from the textbook: "John's secretary makes coffee in the morning." She read the sentence as crisply as a prosecutor putting her case to a court. "Why not use this sentence instead?"

"John's secretary makes coffee in the morning." It was a grammatical sentence. But then so was "Here is the secretary of bees." And without any of the textbook's blandness. Only the latter induced the students' attention. I spoke carefully.

"The textbook's sentence is, shall we say, factual. It contains a lot of facts. There is someone called John; John has a secretary; the secretary makes coffee; the coffee is made in the morning. One fact after another and another. They make no pictures. Everything is simply assumed. The world is the world. And in the world Johns have secretaries, and secretaries make coffee, and coffee is drunk in the morning."

"What wrong with that?" the director demanded. Her accent was Russian.

"Memory—for one thing. Lots of facts go forgotten. No fact, no word. The student's language becomes full of gaps. Whereas the other kind of sentence is different; it doesn't assume anything. It's not a fact; it's a picture. The students can imagine what a secretary of bees would look like. And imagining, they understand and remember better."

As I spoke, I sensed that the director and I had irreconcilable differences concerning how a language ought to be taught. Even so, she heard me out. I said that each word in a textbook, being a fact, could mean more or less only one thing. A word in a poem, on the other hand, could say ten different things. When Plath writes of hearing someone's speech "thick as foreign coffee," *coffee* here means so much more than it does in the hands of John's docile secretary. The line stimulates the reader's interest. *Thick* and *foreign* are lent an aura of unfamiliarity. Questions begin to multiply. How can a word be thick (or thin)? Why describe the coffee as foreign? Were the words Plath heard like coffee because they were bitter? Did they give her black thoughts? So that instead of repeating a word—*coffee* or *thick* or *foreign*—ten times over in ten different sentences ("Can I have a cup of coffee please?," "My favorite drink is coffee," "His wife is foreign," "This cinema shows foreign films every other week"), hammering it into the memory, the same word can be understood in ten different ways in a single reading and absorbed instantly.

For the director, poetry was only a side effect of language, peripheral; for me it was essential. A student would learn phrases like "arrange hair" or "arrange an appointment" far more easily, I thought, after reading Plath's line "Arranging my morning." Not the other way around. Grammar and memory come from playing with words, rubbing them on the fingers and on the tongue, experiencing the various meanings they give off. Textbooks are no substitute.

The director relented. It wasn't as if she could fire me; labor cannot get any cheaper than free. But before I went, she had a job she needed doing. The European Union money on which the center depended for its annual budget was fast disappearing; and in order to acquire new funds, the director had drafted in English a project proposal that she wanted me to look over. I read the printout. The old Soviet way with words! Bureaucratese. Syntax minus meaning—every second word replaceable, every third or fourth dispensable. An Amstrad's pride. What could I tell her? I thought of my students. I bit my lip and said it should be fine.

Wednesday evenings we were usually five or six at my apartment: me, Birutė, Aida, and two or three of the other students. Conversation practice. These no-pressure sessions over tea were my way of reciprocating the women's regular gifts of food and advice and hospitality, and the respect with which they dealt with me, a young man — young enough to be, for some of them, a son — living alone in the snowy depths of a post-Soviet country, a thousand miles from his family. To Lithuanians, Birutė confided one sleety evening, such informal gatherings were still rather new; they had only in recent years started to forget to close their curtains, to talk without fearing walls with ears, and to not jump when a drunken neighbor bangs at the wrong door. I discovered then why the apartment, which had been vacant for some time before my coming, contained no books.

During the decades of Soviet occupation, an army of censors had stalked Lithuanian for the tiniest inkling of protest, of satire, of ambiguity. Back then every word was a potential suspect, every misprint a potential crime. Up and down the country, millions of books were hauled away from homes and pulped. Book inspectors could turn up on your doorstep at all hours. Why is this Cyrillic-print paperback propping up a table? How come Comrade Stalin's *Dialectical and Historical Materialism* sits in your bathroom? Who spilt tea on the novel (by an author awarded a state prize) here? In this climate of trepidation many readers chose to take precautionary steps. Children's books, Russian-language bestsellers, popular stories and novellas, and even works signed Vladimir Lenin were all fed to stoves. It would take days, sometimes weeks, for the odor of vanished words to lift.

What a difference, then, for the women who freely fraternized every Wednesday evening, the five or six of us speaking English (and me, my best Lithuanian) to our heart's content. Cradling the poetry anthology on her knees, one of the students, like an inexperienced reader, would turn the pages gingerly and read a few lines or verses aloud. Then the others would describe a memory that the picture made by the words had dislodged. Sometimes the women's memories were of nursery rhymes they had learned as a little girl from a mother or grandmother. Lithuanian words of course, but the same sorts of rhymes, the same rhythms. The iambic beat of the heart.

> *Musė maišė, musė maišė,* [*"The fly mixed, the fly mixed"*]
> *uodas vandens nešė,* [*"The mosquito carried water,"*]
> *saulė virė, saulė virė,* [*"The sun boiled, the sun boiled,"*]
> *mėnesėlis kepė.* [*"The little moon baked."*]

It was Aida, if I remember rightly, who sang. She might have been our mother, gently lulling her children to sleep. Her voice was warm and soft.

It was not unusual for my apartment to ring with the nation's songs and sayings, for the English the women conversed in was often supplemented by Lithuanian puns, asides, exclamations. They were like the compositions I taught in class. In a little notebook, I entered my gleaned favorites, with the odd doodle of a comment:

"Buckle rhymes with night: sagtis/naktis. Think 'black buckle.'"

"Rankų darbo sidabro (handmade silver) — said when describing a wedding ring. Similar effect in handmade diamond."

"Crust on bread is 'pluta' — froth on beer is 'puta' — 'alus be putos, duona be plutos' (beer without froth, bread without crust) = 'good as nothing.'"

"Nettles are compared to wolves: they bite. 'Wolf' = vilkas, which rhymes with šilkas (silk). Glossy leaves. Nettles — nets — threads."

The flashes of native wit elated me; the words of a riddle or proverb could make my Wednesday. They were the words of Lithuanian's infancy, the forefathers around fires, faces lit up and colored amber — words so musical and picturesque that I listened and blinked with pleasure. They made me wonder who was truly the language teacher — the women or I? They seemed to me to be troves of knowledge. Inestimable.

In April, the last of the snow turned to slush, then to water, then to an increasingly distant memory. *Snow* — and its Lithuanian counterpart, *sniegas* — returned to the dictionary to estivate. The Wednesdays were getting longer; the women arrived at my apartment looking less tired, and stayed later. They read the poems aloud and spoke in English more easily. Assurance rejuvenated them, made their skin shine. I had never seen the women look as beautiful as they did then.

Two months later my class broke up for the summer. After making my goodbyes at the center, I had a little time on my hands before the flight home. Birutė, considerate Birutė, took me to the theater. As luck would have it, a Lithuanian-language production of *My Fair Lady* (*Mano puikioji ledi*) was running. I hadn't read the original play; I hadn't seen the film or musical. Everything—the songs, the set, the curious clothes—was new to me. Or nearly. Halfway through the spectacle, my reserve of patience ebbing since the actors rushed their lines, or so I imagined, all of a sudden I found I understood:

"Daug lietaus Ispanijoje!"

"The rain in Spain stays mainly in the plain."

Triumph was in the young actress's voice. She repeated the line, as if savoring every word.

"Daug lietaus Ispanijoje!"

I could hardly contain my joy.

Three

YOU ARE WHAT YOU SAY

The first time I met with scientists eager to examine the goings-on of my mind, I was given a vocabulary test. Fifteen years on, I still remember how my heart sank. I had volunteered for their research with the intention of talking, explaining, recounting—of condensing my multicolored thoughts, my unusual (as I had been told) creative processes, into words. I had never had that conversation before, could scarcely wait to have it (though, as it happened, the wait would ultimately grow by three more years). Before leaving for central London and the psychology department there, not knowing the sorts of test that lay in store for me, I had made a mental inventory of what I hoped to find: television-handsome doctors, open ears and open minds, answers to my zillion questions. I was prodigiously naive. My disappointment was almost immediate. No sooner had I arrived than I contemplated turning on my heels and taking the next underground train back. The whitecoats asked only for my age, my school grades, whether I was left- or right-handed. Then, they gestured toward a thin, impassive lady who led me down a narrow corridor. The woman introduced where we were going and rattled off a list of rote instructions to follow. I was told to speak clearly because her pen would record my every error. A taker of tests, that was all the people here saw in me. But I was too intimidated to back out. And so, once I had been shown into a low-ceilinged, white-walled rabbit-cage of a room, the vocabulary test began.

Fifty words, printed on a foolscap sheet, which I was to read aloud one by one. Clearing my throat gave me enough time to take in a surprising pattern in the list of words: quite a few of them—*aisle, psalm, debt* (as in "forgive us our debts, as we forgive our debtors"), *catacomb, zealot, leviathan, beatify, prelate, campanile*—had to do with the Church. And there were, it seemed to me, further clues to the identity of the person behind the list. Medical words—*ache, nausea, placebo, puerperal*—suggested a doctor. Still others—*bouquet, cellist, topiary*—hinted at a life far removed from the East End factories and pound shops of my own childhood.

"*Chord*," I muttered to the invigilator. It was the first word on the list.

"Please go on," she said. Her voice was glassy.

I wanted to say, "It is a golden word. Gold, white, and red. Like the colors of the flag of Nunavut. And if you retype the word in small letters, reordering them to spell *dcorh,* and then trim the tops off the tall letters, the *d* and the *h,* do you see the anagram *acorn?*" But I didn't say any of this.

"Please go on," she said again. My responses came reluctantly.

Some words later, when I reached *equivocal,* I stopped and let out a small gasp, which was like laughter. *Equivocal!* A green word, a shiny word. A word comprising each of the five vowels. So beautiful. I was beside myself with enthusiasm. But the woman with the glassy voice didn't seem to notice. *Equivocal!* A word cool to the touch. The greenness. The shininess. The coolness. They all came at me simultaneously. The word radiated the sea on a late British summer afternoon—the briny, occasionally garlicky, smell of the sea—and aroused a momentary nostalgia for the coast. *Equivocal,* lifting my mood, offering me color and beauty in the ambient drabness—suddenly made my coming here seem worth the trouble. Even if I had to reduce it to a game of pronunciation, to four syllables with accent on the second.

Much of my learning had come from library books. If I could recognize *prelate* and *beatify* (though I was unchurched, and my parents nonbelievers), knew that *gaoled* was an olde worlde way of spelling *jailed,* and was able to place *quadruped* as the Latin for *four-footed,* it was because of all the years I'd spent around assorted dictionaries and encyclopedias. But the one-sidedness of this instruction had its limits, something the test would now proceed to amply demonstrate. *"Aeon."* It brought me to a halt. From this word forward, I apprehended the certainty of fumbles. While understandable enough in print, "aeon" was a sound that I could only vaguely make. A-on? Air-on? E-on? It was like a shibboleth, like pronouncing Lord Cholmondeley as "chumly," or Magdalen College, Oxford, as "maud-lin." You had to be in the know.

You are what you say. But this notion of "verbal intelligence"—so dear to the box-tick-happy psychologist—that language is something you can measure precisely and put an exact number on, struck me as false. And the list that had been compiled by this notion contained some kind of assessment. What was it? What action, I wondered, what social task might ever require me to say something like *drachm* (and pronounce it "dram")? It was hard to dispel my doubts. The dubiety ran deep in me. I knew from my days at school that obscure and rare words—"dictionary words"—spoiled dialogue more often than not and banished their user to solitude. The experience had not been easy on me.

And yet I didn't speak my mind. I was to regret that afterward. But looking back, I can understand. Just what could I have said, assuming that I would have even been granted a hearing? That simply knowing a word like *drachm*, its pronunciation, did not make you a better, more intelligent, speaker? That listing words on their own, denuded of context and meaning, was impoverishing? That language, that feeling and thinking and creating in language, bore no resemblance to so pointless and inane an exercise? But the men and women here were psychologists, with the brisk deskside manners and the degrees of psychologists. Who was I to say anything? I, a twenty-two-year-old, underemployed man. Parents, a former sheet-metal worker and a stay-at-home mom. Higher education, none (at that time) to speak of. Obediently, I kept my head down and stuck to reading the list through to the end.

I remember now that there was a moment of confusion

over the final item on the list. *"Campanile."* I said it in the French way, *à la française.* I had learned French at school; during my teens I'd had French pen pals; I had holidayed one summer at the home of a family in Nantes. So I had a good accent. But the invigilator hesitated; she raised her free hand to her bell-bottomed black hair. And let it drop. "No," she said at last, since it was time for the debriefing, and added *"Campanile* comes from Italy." Cam-pa-nee-lee, she said, with what she insisted was the correct pronunciation. It was what her notes told her. I started to object, but checked myself and let it pass. Another concession. According to the online version of the *Oxford English Dictionary*, either way of saying the word is right.

After a few other tests (equally mind-numbing, like having a story read to me and being asked to recall it), I left and never went back to the department. I never heard from its staff again. But whenever, in the years that followed, I came across one of those newspaper or magazine advertisements for "word power packs"—"At the Crucial Moments of Your Life, Do Your Words Fail You? Give yourself the chance to become the articulate man who succeeds in business...the fluent man who enjoys a rich social life...the facile speaker who is esteemed by his community"—it would remind me of that wasted day in central London and the psychologist with the glassy voice. The smudgy shill in the ad, the white-coats' picture of articulateness in his thick-framed glasses and three-piece suit, appeared inches across from the pitches of scalp specialists and Positive Thinkers. A Get-Glib-Quick scheme. I didn't buy it. But the message continues to seduce to this day. The salesmen understand their buyers, the complexes of working-class vocabulary, the desire of many to improve themselves. They charge a few cents for every ten-dollar word and make you believe you've got yourself a bargain.

I'm not divulging any great trade secrets if I tell you these "word power packs" don't work. The associations they teach, like the vocabulary test's list, seem pointlessly artificial. Take, for instance, the cousin of *timid* and SAT favorite, *timorous* ("timorous, *adj.*: Full of or affected by fear"). Instead of picturing a Tim Burton movie, or the British tennis choker Tim Henman, better to read from the poem "To a Mouse," by Robert Burns:

Wee, sleekit, cowrin, tim'rous beastie,
O, what a panic's in thy breastie!

As a teenager, that was how I learned the adjective: I let the poet's imagery animate it for me. The learning did not cost me a penny; and I suppose if it had, I would have been sore as hell at the seller, because not once have I heard or said it since. Most native English speakers seem to get happily by with *afraid* or *frightened* or *fearful,* or even, in the north of the United Kingdom, *frit.* Few, if any, have ever found themselves short a *timorous.*

Even as a very young man, I had certain intuitions about language being irreducible to individual pieces of vocabulary. But for a long time that was all they were. My thoughts needed clarifying. But I couldn't rush them. After my diagnosis at 25 — high-functioning autistic savant syndrome ("with excellent adaptation in adulthood") and synesthesia, big words in their own right — I traveled, I read, I wrote. I became a writer. Time and experience did their work: clarity gradually came to me. Two things helped my thinking in particular. The first and biggest, almost ten years after reading aloud *aeon* and *drachm* and *campanile,* was my decision, upon entering my thirties, to finally study at a university. Remembrance of that list, of not speaking my mind out of self-consciousness or lack of social skill or confidence, niggled and played its part in prompting me to put a portion of my author royalties into a bachelor of arts degree. Among my other courses in the humanities, I chose sociolinguistics and discovered in it, like a revelation, the work of Shirley Brice Heath.

A sociolinguist and ethnographer, too little known in her native United States, Shirley Brice Heath concluded as early as the 1970s that schoolchildren from different social classes and cultures were set apart academically, not by deficits in IQ or vocabulary size, but by the differing "ways with words" in which they were raised. Heath, who has risen to the academic stratosphere at Stanford, is a former foster daughter of a milkman and a factory employee. She is passionate about her studies in language development and child literacy. Her painstaking fieldwork, in the Piedmont Carolinas, took close to ten years to complete. With the chameleon qualities of a born anthropologist, Heath lived, talked, and played with the children and their relatives and acquaintances in two neighboring textile mill communities: one

("Roadville") white, the other ("Trackton") black. She compared her findings with the behaviors of young "Maintown" families like her own, white and middle class, whose children had doctors and professors for parents. In all three groups, Heath showed, the children grew up speaking a rich, fully-formed American English; only the manner in which they attained that fluency and the uses to which they put their English differed.

Maintown parents, Heath noted, treated even toddling sons and daughters as their conversational equals. "School-oriented," the parents behaved much like teachers, accompanying a bedtime story with bright-voiced explanations of the narrative, riffs on theme and character, and little quizzes, concocted on the spot, to assist (and assess) the child's comprehension. By the time the child began school, classroom decorum came more or less naturally. The pupil had appropriate responses to Mr. Brown's or Mrs. Cooper's questions down pat.

In Roadville, boys and girls learned to read whatever picture books their parents' dollars could stretch to buy; but, contrary to their peers in Maintown, come reading time, they fidgeted. The books, picked out from grocery checkout stands, quite often failed to hold the attention of either party for very long, making the experience a chore. Parental explanations of a narrative tended to be perfunctory. No riffs, then. No little quizzes. Instead, the children would mostly hear stories by listening to adults "tell on" themselves for laughs among friends, family, or townsfolk. A Roadville story was typically a story that diligently recounted a past event and held some kind of moral: storytelling in the normal sense was considered tantamount to lying. If asked by the schoolteacher to write a story about coming down from outer space or levitating in the air, the Roadville-raised pupil would hardly even know where to start.

Trackton's preschoolers were hardly ever addressed directly by adults. As one grandmother explained it, "Ain't no use me tellin' 'im: learn this, learn that, what's this, what's that? He just gotta learn, gotta know; he see one thing one place one time, he know how it go, see sump'n like it again, maybe it be the same, maybe it won't." But there was no speech delay. The infants learned as if by osmosis. Many became uncanny mimics, able to reproduce the walk and talk of family, neighbors, and regular visitors down to the gas meter man. Trackton talk was more allusive than that heard in the other communities: listeners were expected to mentally fill in any gaps. Impromptu stories had no formulaic "once upon a time" beginnings or verbal wrappings-up to signal the end—the narratives ran on analogy, leaping from one thought or incident to another, and lasted however long audiences would entertain them. Schoolteachers often found pupils from Trackton boisterous (or else withdrawn) in class and less ruly in their compositions, finding in a lesson parallels that might not have been intended.

In 1983, Heath published her findings. She urged teachers to ponder the background of every pupil and their Maintown biases carefully. Too often, red pens penalized Roadville and Trackton students' different ways with words, mistaking them for deficiencies; the bar of academic ambition was correspondingly lowered. Abandoned to their frustration, their incomprehension, class laggers found themselves relegated to the shock of remedial lessons from which their young confidence frequently never recovered.

Such a waste! And yet, more than thirty years after Heath's publication, the cruel circle remains intact. As an ideological shortcut, the equation of poverty with poverty of thought is as popular as ever. Media and lawmakers fret that the less well-off are "word poor." Nothing, though, could be further from the truth. As Curt Dudley Marling, a professor in the Lynch School of Education at Boston College, writes, "All children come to school with extraordinary linguistic, cultural, and intellectual resources, just not the *same* resources. . . . Respect for students' knowledge, who they are, where they come from . . . is the key to successful teaching." Indeed, in those schools where children's differences have been roundly welcomed, their particular strengths nurtured (and weaknesses thoughtfully attended to), poorer pupils demonstrate just as supple an attention and just as ravenous an appetite for words, stories, and puzzles as other students do.

Shirley Brice Heath's linguistic anthropology fed my understanding of language. So, too, did my encounter with the work of a young American lexicographer, Erin McKean. In her various media appearances, widely relayed on the Internet, her slogan — *if a word works, use it* — struck home. I liked what she had to say about modern dictionaries, that they map a language and explore every nook and cranny of its well- and lesser-trod acres; that they avoid the snobbery of their older counterparts: high culture's doormen charged with excluding all words they judge "bad," "uncouth," or "incorrect." And I liked how, in keeping with her colorful published guide to the semiotics of dresses (her other passion), McKean's sole editorial criterion is whether this or that word "fits," whether its form and the speaker's (or author's) purpose sufficiently "match."

McKean says she always wanted to be a lexicographer, ever since she read about one in a newspaper as a kid. She started out doing manuscript annotation ("a fancy word for 'underlining with colored pencils'") for the Chicago Assyrian Dictionary, before landing positions consecutively at Thorndike-Barnhart Children's Dictionaries, and the American Dictionaries division for Oxford University Press. In 2004, only thirty-three, she was tapped to become *New Oxford American Dictionary*'s editor in chief. But lexicography has evolved so rapidly since then that she now works exclusively online, having come to the conclusion that "books are the wrong containers for dictionaries." The nonprofit *Wordnik,* which McKean launched in 2009, is billed as the world's biggest online dictionary. It forages for words within meaningful phrases and sentences on the Internet and in the contents of millions of digitized books going back centuries: words that, for want of space or knowledge of their existence, appear in no print dictionary, no vocabulary list, no SAT test. *Wordnik* includes never-before-documented words such as *slenthem* (a Javanese musical instrument) and *deletable.* The resulting map of English, its boundaries expanding by the day, is like no other; it is

changing how we define *English,* since — on the conservative estimations of data scientists — the lexicon is more than
twice as big as anyone ever previously imagined.

"My biggest frustration is not having enough hours in the
day to do all the work that I would like to do," writes McKean
in an email. "Although (going by the actuarial tables) I'm
barely halfway through my expected lifespan, it's more likely
than not that I will die before *Wordnik* is 'finished' — the
nature of the lexicography is that most lexicographers don't
live to see the culmination of their projects, because English
never stops and so the projects never really end."

"English never stops." It could be McKean's motto. Every
minute of every hour of every day, someone in the English-
speaking world plays a new combination of sounds, letters,
and meanings on a listener or reader. Who, understanding,
nods. English! Only tweaked, stretched, renewed. Words —
but also what we talk about when we talk about words — are
constantly shifting. When I clicked on *Wordnik*'s "random
search" option, "to-dos," the eminently logical plural of
"to-do," popped up. Intrigued, I performed a quick side
search on the Internet and turned up a 2001 *New York
Times* article featuring "not-to-dos." Back on *Wordnik,* I
clicked again:

"'Nonfraud, *adj.* Not of or pertaining to fraud': 'The SEC
alleges that Assurant violated certain nonfraud-related sec-
tions of the Securities Exchange Act of 1934 with the
accounting of this reinsurance contract' (from a 2010 article
in *Insurance Journal*)."

And once more:

"'Goaltend, *v.* To engage in goaltending': 'Saturday afternoon, we were certain that...NBA commissioner David Stern would plop atop the Orlando rim and goaltend all of Rashard Lewis's three-point attempts' (from a 2009 article in *The Wall Street Journal*)."

Predictably enough, some of McKean's correspondents, particularly those fondest of the Caps Lock key, will complain that a *Wordnik* entry "isn't a word, because it isn't a word that they like." The pedants' *grr*ing is a smaller frustration, since she knows she cannot reason with her critics. Better to save her attention for mail like the enthusiastic message that came last Christmas from a class of Australian schoolchildren, proposing their own (and who knows, perhaps impending) words, such as *insaniparty, kerbobble,* and *melopink.*

McKean's own English, her own "way with words," doesn't seem all that much like the English of a lexicographer (though, apparently, her son's is that of a lexicographer's child: at the age of six he wrote — and without a letter out of place — *discombobulated* in his first-grade class journal). She can tweet, "just fyi, if I ever 'snap' it will be 100% caused by someone loudly popping their chewing gum on public transit." She is not above typing *gonna* and *gotta; lookupable* (as in "every word should be lookupable"), *made-upical,* and *undictionaried* are all words of her invention, and in her sentences they read just fine. ("Words only have meaning in context," she notes. "If I just say 'toast' to you, you don't know if you're getting strawberry jam or champagne.")

*   *   *

"Chord." "Drachm." "Aeon." "Campanile." What, I still wonder, did the psychologist listening believe she understood? You are what you say—well, maybe, up to a point. Every voice carries certain personality traits—the tongue-tiedness of one; of another, the overreaching vowels. Every voice, in preferring *dinner* to *supper,* or in pronouncing *this* as *dis,* betrays traces of its past. But vocabulary is not destiny. Words, regardless of their pedigree, make only as much sense as we choose to give them. We are the teachers, not they. To possess fluency, or "verbal intelligence," is to animate words with our imagination.

Every word is a bird we teach to sing.

Four

A POET SAVANT

The Australian poet Les Murray makes life hard for those who wish to describe him. It isn't only his work, which has been put out in some thirty books over a period of fifty years, and which, having won major literary prize after major literary prize, has made its author a perennial candidate for a Nobel. It is the man. In PR terms, Murray seems the antipode of Updikean dapperness, cold Coetzee intensity, Zadie Smith's glamour. His author photographs, which appear to be snapshots, can best be described as ordinary. The bald man's hat, the double chin, the plain t-shirt. A recent photograph, accompanying his *New Selected Poems,* shows him at a kitchen table, grandfatherly in his glasses. The artlessness is that of an autodidact. Murray has always written as his own man. Fashions, schools, even the occasional dictionary definition, he serenely flouts. To read him is to know him.

A high hill of photographed sun-shadow
coming up from reverie, the big head
has its eyes on a mid-line, the mouth
slightly open, to breathe or interrupt.

The face's gentle skew to the left
is abetted, or caused, beneath the nose
by a Heidelberg scar, got in an accident.
The hair no longer meets across the head

and the back and sides are clipped ancestrally
Puritan-short. The chins are firm and deep
respectively. In point of freckling
and bare and shaven skin is just over

halfway between childhood ginger
and the nutmeg and plastic death-mottle
of great age. The large ears suggest more
of the soul than the other features:

(These lines are from his "Self-Portrait from a Photograph,"
in *Collected Poems*.)

His is a singular way with words; Murray admits to inter-
viewers that he is something of a "word freak." His linguistic
curiosity is immense, obsessive. *Gnamma* (an Aboriginal
word for desert rock-holes wet with rainwater), the Anglo-
Hindi *kubberdaur* (from the Hindi *khabardaar* meaning "look
out!"), *toradh* (Irish Gaelic for "fruit" or "produce"), *neb*
(Scots for "nose"), *sadaka* ("alms" in Turkish), the German
Leutseligkeit ("affability"), *rzeczpospolita* (what Poland, in its
red-tape documents, calls itself), *halevai* (a Yiddish exclamation): these are just a few of the many exotic words that
Murray, over the years, has lavished on his poetry. "His

genius," reported *The Australian*, "is an ability to process the 1,025,000 words in his brain and select precisely the right one to follow the one that came before it." The estimate is the reporter's — an unfortunate piece of silliness in an otherwise serious article. The estimate — not something to consider, something only to gawp at — comes from old attitudes, still publishable in 2014, toward "freaks" like Murray.

Murray, as the same article notes, lives with high-functioning autism.

I discovered Les Murray in the early 2000s (a short while before my own high-functioning autism diagnosis). It happened in an English bookshop. The bookshop was in Kent, my home at the time. It was a large shop, bright with snazzy book covers, and superintended by a discreet staff. It welcomed browsers. Every now and then I came into the shop and thumbed its wares and pretended to have money. The pretense did me good. It taught me the prospective book buyer's graces. In the poetry section one day, I was looking at the stock — short books written by long names like Annette von Droste-Hülshoff, Guillaume de Saluste Du Bartas, Keorapetse Kgositsile, Wisława Szymborska — when a cover that bore the surprisingly modest name of Les Murray caught my eye. The familiarity of that "Les," its ungentlemanliness, so seemingly out of place in a poetry section, appealed to me. And the book's title was as intriguing as the author's name was likable: *Poems the Size of Photographs*. I picked it up and read. And read. It was the first time I read a book from cover to cover while standing in the shop. It helped, of course, that the pages, compared to a novel's or a biography's, were fairly few, and many of the hundred-odd poems rather short. Short, occasionally, to the point of evoking haiku-like riddles:

> This is the big arrival.
> The zipper of your luggage
> Growls *valise* round three sides
> And you lift out the tin clothes.

Short or long, each of the poems had something to pique my interest. The word pictures were vivid and felt right: magpies wore "tailcoats," which, at the faintest noise, broke "into wings"; headstones complete with crosses were the "marble chess of the dead"; in a house, "air [had] sides." And Murray's patent delight in language, his fascination with it, matched mine. He wrote like a man for whom language was something strange, and strangely beautiful. "Globe globe globe globe" is Murray mimicking a jellyfish. A soda bottle a little girl taps against her head, Murray informs the reader with onomatopoeic precision, sounded "boinc." "Bocc" was the bottle's response when it struck the side of a station wagon. A woman could simultaneously describe a cheese in Australian English and, with copious gesturing, in "body Italian." And in the modern landscape of ever-present signs — airport signs, road signs, door signs, computer signs — the poet saw a "World language" of pictographs, a language that could be "written and read, even painted but not spoken." He imagined its vocabulary:

Good is thumbs up, thumb and finger zipping lips
  is *confidential*. *Evil* is three-cornered snake eyes.
    . . .
  Two animals in a book read *Nature,* two books.
  Inside an animal, *instinct*. Rice in bowl with chop-
sticks denotes *food*. Figure 1 lying prone equals *other*.

Every pictograph would be findable, definable, in a
"square-equals-diamond book," a dictionary.

I wanted very much to buy Murray's book. But I had no
money. I had to wait. At my next birthday I came into a
small sum, my age in pounds sterling, and spent it on the
poems.

Without Murray's poems, I might never have become a
writer. At the time, so early in my adulthood, their oddness
reassured. I could see myself in them. In London, my
English had never been the English of my parents, siblings,
or schoolmates; my sentences — oblique, wordy, allusive —
had led to mockery, and the mockery had caused my voice to
shrink. But Murray's was sprawling; it held a hard-won ease
with how its words behaved. If I had known then what I
finally confirmed years later, that this poet's voice, so beautiful and so skillful, was autistic, and that Murray was an
autistic savant, I might have seen myself differently. I might
have written my essays and my first novel and my own poetry
years before they finally made their way into print. But
nobody told me; and what was only a hunch, after being
diagnosed myself, that Murray too had autism, remained
only that. Happily, this hunch was enough to restore

confidence in my own voice, to nourish it back up to size. My voice eventually grew as big as a book: a memoir of my autistic childhood.

Only while writing my second book—a survey of scientific ideas about the brain—did I learn why no doctor or researcher would have told me that this famous poet (and more than a poet, one of the English language's great men of letters) was autistic. It wasn't due to lack of candor or self-awareness on the poet's part. As early as the 1970s Murray wrote, in a poem entitled "Portrait of the Autist as a New World Driver," of belonging to the "loners, chart-freaks, bush encyclopaedists...we meet gravely as stiff princes, and swap fact" (a pity it was only collected thirty years later, and brought to my attention quite recently); in several more recent newspaper profiles, he described himself as a "high-performing Asperger" (a pity, too, I didn't see these at the time). The reason, I discovered, was that most scientists thought autism inhospitable to creativity, especially the literary kind. Their attitudes were colored by having studied a very particular type of savant: those with a low or lowish IQ, nonverbal or mumbling. I pressed the scientists I met or wrote to. Had they really never heard of any autistic person with a gift for words? They had, I was told, and his name was Christopher. Christopher, in the photographs I saw, was coy and pasty, mustached and middle-aged, a Briton with brain damage, who spent his days turning the pages of his impressive collection of Teach Yourself books. Reading nearly around the clock he had taught himself, to varying extents, some twenty languages. And yet Christopher couldn't write.

In the end, it was Murray's following release, *The Biplane Houses*, that turned my hunch to certainty. By that time I had left Kent and its bookshop and was living in the south of France. I ordered my copy in a click of Internet: it arrived in a many-stamped airmail envelope—a small, slender, red and white book looking none the worse for the cross-channel journey. As I flipped through the poems, I read, in the form of a sonnet, not a declaration of love, but the author's contemplation of his mind:

Asperges me hyssopo
the snatch of plainsong went,
Thou sprinklest me with hyssop
was the clerical intent,
not Asparagus with hiccups
and never autistic savant.

Asperger, mais. Asperg is me.
The coin took years to drop:

Lectures instead of chat. The want
of people skills. The need for Rules.
Never towing a line from the Ship of Fools.
The avoided eyes. Great memory.
Horror not seeming to perturb—
Hyssop can be a bitter herb.

I had read in who knows how many scientific papers that people with autism took up language—even twenty varieties—merely to release it as echoes. So I was thrilled to see Murray's lines, full of wit and feeling and prowess, prove their theories wrong. They made me want to learn all about the man behind the pen. I went to my computer; I punched in the poet's name and autism; the resulting webpages were many, well stocked, enlightening. The information had been there all along. But the reporters had pushed it to the margins. Each had written about Murray's autism only briefly, sketchily, as something that didn't fit. They had not thought to look any further, to look at the poet's oeuvre or his life in another light. To learn this side of Murray's story I had to piece it together by myself, click by click and link by link, following up every byte of every source that I could verify. Slowly, scattered facts took on the vivid colors of anecdote; interview digressions lost their blur. The developed picture of the poet's early life—the many years his mind took to adjust to language—was as revealing as it was compelling.

Leslie Allan Murray was born in 1938 in Nabiac, a small bush town and inland port in dairy farming country, 175 miles northeast of Sydney. His ancestors, agricultural laborers, had sailed from the Southern Uplands of Scotland in the mid-nineteenth century, bringing with them their Presbyterian faith and Scots dialect: *fraid* for a "ghost," *elder* for "udder."

Les was an only child. From his first shriek, the baby's senses overworked: his indigent parents' weatherboard house frequently trembled with tantrums. Nothing but a warm bath in water heated on the boxwood-burning stove and then poured, crackling, into a galvanized washtub could soothe him.

The house was poky. There wasn't room for homebodies. Life was in the main outdoors — on the outskirts of the house, the white of sheep, the black of hens, the green of paddocks. The little boy imitated the calls of willie wagtails and played with cows and crows. He rambled by himself the hilly hectares around the settlement, returning at dusk soaked as if in a cloudburst of perspiration.

Very early, he learned the alphabet from canned-food labels. He took at once to reading the few books around the home: the Aberdeen-Angus studbook, the *Yates Seed Catalogue*, the Alfa Laval cream separator manual, and all eight volumes of the 1924 edition of *Cassell's Book of Knowledge*. The books and he became the best of friends. He slept with them every night out on the veranda.

There were no educational establishments for miles, so when Les was seven, school started going to him. The postman was the intermediary. The lessons by correspondence — in handwriting, grammar, and arithmetic — came every week, postmarked from Sydney, and the boy delighted in tracing pothooks, building phrases, and solving sums at a kitchen table surrounded by buckets and chips of wood.

Two years later, and three and a half miles away, a fifteen-pupil school opened. Les decided he could not go there empty-handed; he asked his mother for several sheaths of white kraft paper, and with a regularly resharpened pencil

wrote a long essay about the Vikings (the information courtesy of volume eight of his encyclopedia). The helmeted berserkers, the swishing axes, the longboats: no historical detail
was too small. He lost himself in the writing. After trekking
off at dawn and arriving hours later, he read his work aloud
to the class: both short- and long-winded. Les was lucky in
his teacher. Just out of graduate school, the teacher hadn't
had enough experience to classify the boy as odd. Les's essay
was patiently listened to; its precocious author thanked.
Then Les and the fourteen other pupils were told to open
their textbooks to page one.

He was more or less left to his own devices and soon
drifted away from class and sequestered himself in the
school's bookroom. With the exception of a few cousins,
amiable and of similar age, he much preferred the company
of books to other children. But even with the cousins Les
wasn't much of a talker. If he wasn't talked to, he wouldn't
start. When the boys induced him to play with them, it was
only by going along with his obsessions. His greatest was the
war: he had been a child of the war, and though incomprehensible, *war,* he knew, meant something excitingly big and
far away, a silencer of grown-ups, about which the wireless
had gone on and on in quick, breathy voices. So the cousins
agreed to play Germans. Along the rabbit-ridden creek they
raced and leapt and hid. Les spoke to them in orders. He
tried sounding German; it made sense to him that he should
try. Compared to the other boys, he had always felt and
seemed somewhat foreign.

His mother died when he was twelve. Her widower's sobbing was incessant. It could be heard by the son, lying beneath several bedcovers, in the veranda. Les hadn't known his father could make such sounds. He interrupted his learning to attempt to grieve too. But what came so naturally to his father mystified him: crying was something he couldn't get the hang of. He grieved with his feet instead of his eyes, tramping them red, crisscrossing the valley until every fence-post hole, every patch of gravel, every spot, to a blade of grass, was part of him. So that whenever distress tightened his stomach and threatened tears, he closed his eyes and called up the texture of a pebble here, the color of the earth there, and journeyed mile after mile in his head until composure settled on him.

A year taller, he returned to school. It was a bigger school, farther away (he rode the town's milk truck to its gates) with a bigger bookroom. The books soothed. And it helped that the room was not frequented by many children. His desire to keep to himself was as strong as at primary school. When the bookroom closed for lunch, he waited out the break, impatiently. With his back to a playground wall, shyness and anxiety pinning him there, he surveilled the kicking, skipping shadows as they passed.

Taree High, where Les boarded during the week, was rougher. Tall and large for sixteen, he was an easy target of mockery. To every fashion, every norm of appearance, the country boy was oblivious: he stood out from the students' well-laundered clothes and up-to-the-minute hairdos as a bumpkin. Class toughs and teases regularly turned on him, harassed him, pelted him with taunts. He could hardly open his mouth without being laughed at; he spoke like a walking encyclopedia, pedantic. He used—sometimes, misused— long, obscure words: once threatening to "transubstantiate" a taunter through a wall.

Most of the teachers didn't turn a hair to help. But they were dazzled by the sweep and precision of Les's knowledge, by the nonchalance with which a mention of, say, the pre-Columbians in an art lesson might cause him to hold forth on the Aztecs, Zapotecs, Toltecs, and Totonacs. And Mr. McLaughlin, the English teacher, a mild school counselor of limitless patience, was understanding. To teach Les was to be assured of an eager hearing. He was a quick learner. It was Mr. McLaughlin who introduced Les to poetry. Eliot. Hopkins. Les was entranced by Gerard Manley Hopkins's words, tried them out on his tongue. *For skies of couple-colour as a brinded cow.* He read on. Repeated. *With swift, slow; sweet, sour; adazzle, dim.* He knew this and, before long, each of his teacher's other set poems by heart. *Praise Him.* He dreamed of one day composing his own verse.

Les spent the rest of the 1950s in an undergraduate's navy-blue bell bottoms, not the green Dacron overalls he had half-hoped to climb aboard and pilot planes in (the Air Force medical officer failed him on sight). His initial disappointment faded quickly, however, because at Sydney University he discovered a remarkable library—a Gothic, gargoyled sandstone building that seated close to a million books. A million! So he wouldn't feel out of place at the university after all. And then he thought, where will I find the time? He was being serious. Every free hour he had, and quite a few taken ones, went into his reading. He skipped classes and dodged lecturers to skim, scan, browse, peruse. Encyclopedias, poems, novels (baiting boredom — he couldn't enter the domestic scenes or believe the plots), short stories, hymnals, plays. He returned again and again to the *Encyclopaedia Britannica;* he pored over Cicero, Kenneth Slessor, the King James Bible. And then, one day, running the length of a bookcase shelf, a yellow row of Teach Yourself language primers attracted his attention. The exotic letters, words, and sentences enticed. Danish by Hans Anton Koefoed. Russian by Maximilian Fourman. Norwegian by Alf Sommerfelt and Ingvald Marm. French by John Adams. Italian by Kathleen Speight. One after another, in quick succession, Les read them all from end to end. He found them easy. He had the knack of recalling the words, the phrases. And of playing with them, locating rhymes and other patterns, inventing new sentences, freer and more imaginative, out of the authors' dry, stiff examples. To round out his enjoyment, he enrolled for courses in German and preliminary Chinese. In next to no time, a couple of semesters, the languages in which Les could read and write numbered over ten.

Les the reader and linguist flourished; but Les the student floundered. The astringency of the curriculum — read this, not that; write your thesis in this manner, not that — demoralized him. He dropped out, age twenty-one, to see the country; he hitched long rides in trucks. He over-nighted on building sites, in patches of long grass, wherever he could find a dry spot. It was during these vagabond months, in beige, hole-punched notepads, that he wrote his first significant poetry.

He hitchhiked back to Sydney, returned to studentship unsuccessfully, dropping out a second time (he would earn his missing credits only a decade later in 1969), but not before he had met — backstage at a play put on by the German department — his future wife and the future mother of their five children. Usually, with strangers, he couldn't do small talk; conversation would fail him. But with Valerie, to his surprise, he had no such trouble. Valerie, who was born in Budapest and came to Australia after World War II by way of Switzerland, spoke English with a slight Mitteleuro-pean accent. She was a young woman of Hungarian, Swiss-German, and English words. Murray instantly felt at ease with her, and the attraction was mutual. (In 2012 they celebrated their golden wedding anniversary.)

Les's great luck continued. He got a job as a translator for the Australian National University in Canberra. He worked for several departments, rewriting in English one day an Italian paper on "nodular cutaneous diseases in Po Valley hares," the next a Dutch study of the trading history of Makassar. "Languages," in the words of a 1964 newspaper article about the young translator, had become his "bread and butter." For four years he and his growing family lived on Italian and Dutch, German and Afrikaans, French and

Spanish and Portuguese. But it was in English that Murray's poems began to circulate in magazines. They were collected, in 1965, in *The Ilex Tree*. His first literary prize followed. His reputation and his confidence quickly soared. On the strength of the book and prize, he was invited to give readings as far away as Europe. Soon he lost his taste for translating; he left what he would later call his "respectable cover" occupation to write full-time. It was the beginning of one of poetry's most extraordinary careers.

Words have been knots of beauty and mystery as long as I can remember. But Murray's oeuvre was the leaven for my own literary beginnings. So when my debut collection of essays was published several years ago, I dedicated a copy to the poet as a token of gratitude and admiration. But I hesitated before posting it to the bush of New South Wales. What if the book never reached him, or arrived but didn't please him? For a while I couldn't make up my mind. Finally, though, I let my timidity pass. I wrote to the address I had found for Murray in a literary journal, and several weeks later—restless weeks, since each seemed to me to last a month—I had a letter from him.

Time and care had been expended on the letter. Murray's penmanship was firm and fluent (I especially liked his *a*'s, neat little pigtails); the letter was quite long. Far more than a simple thanks then, or even some compliments: the tone throughout was expansive, even confiding. I was touched.

What touched me most was Murray's request that I write again to keep him abreast of my news and my work. An invitation to correspond.

I took him at his word. I wrote. He wrote back. And so it was that letters later, in the course of our now regular correspondence, I proposed to translate a selection of his poems into my second language, French.

I had seen a gap in the international literary market: Murray's poetry, in translation, was already on sale in Berlin bookshops, Moscow libraries, Delhi bazaars. But not, for some strange reason, in the city, a cultural capital, that I had begun to call my home: Paris.

The poet's agent agreed; my editor in Paris agreed. And Murray, in his expansive Australian way, gave me a free hand, carte blanche. I reread the poems, collection after collection after collection; for days, weeks, I immersed myself in them; I ended up selecting forty of my favorites to translate.

Julian Barnes, another Francophile Englishman, has written well of the challenge of translating a literary text. There are, Barnes sighs, as many ways to translate one sentence of a classic as there are translators. In "Translating *Madame Bovary*" he offers, by way of illustration, a straightforward enough line from Flaubert: "aussi poussa-t-il comme un chêne. Il acquit de fortes mains, de belles couleurs," followed by a half-dozen attempts over the years to render the words in convincing English:

"Meanwhile he grew like an oak; he was strong of hand, fresh of color."

"And so he grew like an oak-tree, and acquired a strong pair of hands and a fresh color."

"He grew like a young oak-tree. He acquired strong hands and a good color."

"He throve like an oak. His hands grew strong and his complexion ruddy."

"And so he grew up like an oak. He had strong hands, a good color."

"And so he grew like an oak. He acquired strong hands, good color."

And Flaubert, for all his similes, remains prose, albeit prose of the very highest order. Poetry, by virtue of its nature, is widely thought to be more or less untranslatable (consider Robert Frost's aphorism "poetry is what gets lost in translation").

So translating Murray, I knew, wasn't something to be taken lightly. But I didn't share Frost's limited conception of translation (or of poetry). I could never have rejoiced in Szymborska's ode to the number pi, nor gasped at Mayakovsky's "An Extraordinary Adventure which Befell Vladimir Mayakovsky in a Summer Cottage," had it not been for the ingenuity of their respective translators. All those Polish accents would have scratched my eyes; the black iron gates of Cyrillic would have barred my way. Without translation, some of my favorite works, Bashō's haikus, the Bible's Song of Songs, would have remained beyond reach of my comprehension, forever the preserve of Japanese's and Hebrew's right-to-left readers.

Murray's English is vivid, inventive, jaunty. He is fond of the striking word choice. In recent years the poet has done double duty as an occasional contributor to Australia's *Macquarie Dictionary*. *Pobblebonk* (an informal name for a kind of Australian frog), *doctoring* (the regular seeking of medical assistance), and *Archie* (a World War I anti-aircraft gun) are just a few of his recent submissions. If you read "The Dream of Wearing Shorts Forever," Murray's paean to pants that reach to or almost to the knees, you encounter several amusing stanzas on legwear history and culture, and then these lines:

> To moderate grim vigour
> With the knobble of bare knees

Knobble! I love this poem; it was one of the forty I chose to put into French. I did everything translatorly possible to stay faithful to the text. "Knobble" is Murray's reference to the British (but otherwise little-known) expression "knobbly knees," and I had a hard time coming up with a French equivalent. Knobble. Knobble. I scratched my head. *Bosse?* Bump? *Nœud?* Knot? Neither of these would do. Too abstract. Too neutral. Knobbly knees are funny-looking knees; *knobble* is a funny word. After a lot more head-scratching, I finally hit upon an idea. In place of bump or knot or whatnot could go *tronche*. To French eyes and ears, *tronche* looks and sounds just as comic as *knobble* does to English ones. *Tronche* can mean face (as in "to make a funny face"), expression, the (dodgy, weird, or amusing) look or demeanor of an object or person. *"La tronche!"* is a typical French exclamation, meaning roughly "look at the state of him!" or "get a load of her!" It was as close a parallel as you could get in French. Readers of my translation imagined the stern shirt and tie softened, *par la* (by the) *tronche* (funny face) *des genoux nus* (of bare knees).

Then there is assonance and alliteration, poetry's nuts and bolts. Murray is a master of verse mechanics. "The Trainee, 1914," which was another of my selections, tells of an Australian lured from his hovel to fight in a foreigners' war:

> Till the bump of your drum, the fit of your turned-up hat
> Drew me to eat your stew, salute your flag

Bump, drum; drew, stew; and the end rhyme: *hat, flag.* The poem runs on assonance (there is also similarity of sounds between *fit* and *hat*). All the poetry of the lines resides in these patterns, so in my translation I worked to retain them. I made adjustments. *Bump* became *tempo* (alliterating with *tambour,* the French for "drum"); *fit* turned to *chic* (alliterating with *chapeau,* hat). *Stew* was trickier. What suitable French verbs rhyme with *ragout?* So I had the poem's character eat not stew but *soupe;* and, for the sake of rhyme, tweaked the tense:

> Jusqu'à ce que le tempo de votre tambour, le chic de
>   votre chapeau
> Me poussent à manger votre soupe, à saluer votre
>   drapeau

The hardest thing, of course, was to keep the translations Murray in structure while French in language. Perhaps the most ambitious of my selections, "The Warm Rain" is pure Murray—controlled lines, graphic words, surprising rhymes. Consider the beginning:

> Against the darker trees or an open car shed
> is where we first see rain, on a cumulous day,
> a subtle slant locating the light in air
> in front of a Forties still of tubs and bike-frames.
>
> Next sign, the dust that was white pepper bared
> starts pitting and re-knotting into peppercorns.
> It stops being a raceway of rocket smoke behind cars.

By themselves, these seven lines abound in complexity. If the first two slip fairly smoothly into French,

> Sur un fond d'arbres sombres ou un carport ouvert
> La pluie nous apparaît, un jour nuageux

The others resist. It is necessary to visualize the succession of word pictures as a film. In the third line, the play of raindrops in the air; in the fourth, the shed's exposed interior ("tubs and bike-frames"), by dint of the rainfall, look like something in a grainy "Forties still."

> Des fils subtils [subtle threads] qui rayent et floutent
>   [which scratch and blur] l'air

Comme un retour [like a flashback] sur les années
    quarante [to the Forties] en images.

The beginning of the second stanza, too, shifting focus,
poses difficulties. The imagery is fast-moving, complex.
Dust particles, "white pepper bared," become engorged with
rain and turn to "peppercorns." Ordinarily thrown up by
passing drivers, the puffs of dust "behind cars" no longer
resemble smoke. The translator's task of preserving the allit-
erations, consonance, and assonance from line to line —
"pepper bared," "peppercorns," "behind cars" — is formidable.
Something, in order for my translation to be viable, had to
give. It was the white pepper. I used *sel,* salt, instead.

Puis la terre jusqu'alors fine comme le sel fin
Se mouille et ses particules grossissent en fleur de sel.
Les voitures qui passent n'engendrent plus leur fumée
    de fusil

[Then the earth until then fine-grained as table salt
Grows moist and its particles fatten to *fleur de sel.*
The cars that pass no longer produce their rifle smoke]

Translation takes away, but it also gives. Gone, in French,
are the car shed's tubs and bike frames; gone, also, is the rock-
et's smoke (replaced by a rifle's, to reproduce the pattern of
repeating sounds: "sel fin," "fleur de sel," "leur fumée de fusil").
Two gones, modest losses, but there is a counterbalancing
gain: the French has *fleur de sel;* it more than compensates

with the startling image of a rain that causes the salty earth to flower.

My translation, *C'est une chose sérieuse que d'être parmi les hommes* (*It Is Serious to Be with Humans*), was published in the fall of 2014. On October twelfth, radios tuned in to *France Culture* spoke for thirty minutes in my voice. They told listeners of Murray, his life and work, the repayment of a young writer's debt to his mentor. The broadcast went around the French-speaking world.

Some months later, Murray wrote with pride of a Polynesian neighbor, a native French speaker, who admired the translation and was using it in her French classes. And though his own French was rusty, he said, he could nevertheless understand and enjoy quite a lot. In other letters and postcards—their news ten days older for being sent by snail mail (Murray dislikes computers)—he affectionately recounted long-past trips to Britain, Italy, Germany, and France. But there was nothing in these messages suggesting he might one day return; he hadn't been back in years. He was well into his seventies; his health was unreliable; his farm in Bunyah was over ten thousand miles away.

So the news that he would be in Paris in September 2015 came out of the blue. He had accepted a festival's invitation to speak at la Maison de la Poésie. I was thrilled. Honored, too, when the organizer asked me to share the stage with the poet. Copies of the translation would be on sale after the talk.

Murray, in a multicolored woolly pullover—a dependable "soup-catcher"—braved the twenty-plus hours in an airplane and met me in a bistro. To be able to put a voice, so rich and twangy, to the poems after all this time! At la Maison, the following evening, our conversation had an audience and spotlights and was interspersed with readings in both languages.

After the event, a book signing. The queue was gratifyingly long. I was backstage when someone from the festival came to fetch me; Murray wanted me to sign the book with him.

Murray said, "It's only fair. We're co-authors."

Five

CUECUÈIUCA

Mexico. It means, some say, "center of the world." It was there, in Puebla, the center of the center of the world, that I met an indigene who spoke lightning.

Our meeting took place soon after Día de los Muertos. It wasn't my idea. The day before, jet-lagged, I had had my nose firmly in my notes when one of the conference organizers chaperoning me spotted the book I had taken with me for the plane: *The Nahuas after the Conquest: A Social and Cultural History of the Indians of Central Mexico, Sixteenth Through Eighteenth Centuries* by James Lockhart.

"The *Nawas*," she said, giving me the correct pronunciation of Mexico's largest indigenous group, descendants of the Aztecs, "you are interested in the *Nawas?*"

Who could not be? I thought. I was particularly interested in the Nahuatl ("clear as a bell") language, which has given the Western lexicon *avocado* (*ahuacatl*), *guacamole* (*ahuacamolli*— literally "avocado sauce"), *chocolate* (*xocolatl*), *cacao* (*cacahuatl*), *tomato* (*tomatl*), *chili, chia, peyote* (*peyotl*), *ocelot* (*ocelotl*), and *axolotl* (a type of salamander). "No culture ever took more joy in words," Lockhart writes. No culture ever revered more the power and the magic of sounds. Mexico City (then Tenochtitlán) was always booming, ringing, resounding in the days of Montezuma's glory. The wind whistled, the Aztecs — with flutes and ocarinas — whistled; to the tinkling of a rain shower they added the tinkling of their bracelets, anklets, ceramic pendants and beads; after a night ablare with thunder, a morning of horns and conches, copper gongs and tortoiseshell drums. Singers in iridescent feathers roared like jaguars, squawked like eagles, cooed like quetzals. Mellifluous orations, "flower songs," offered the listener color and beauty, and could inspire and pacify.

My chaperone said, "I know a Nawa man. Quite a talker. He's in town now. I'll arrange a meeting for tomorrow morning, I'll tell him you're only passing through. There's a café close by. I'll write the address down for you. You can meet there."

"Does he speak English?"

"He speaks Spanish. I'll go and telephone him now. Primero Dios, he'll be free."

He was.

His name was Francisco (also his father's name, I learned). He arrived at the café bang on time. His white shirt was spotless and ironed, his brown face was clean-shaven and lively. I bought him coffee and introduced myself as best I could; my Spanish, for want of practice, was a little rough. I said I wanted to learn more about the Nahuatl language.

Nahuatl, he told me (pronouncing it "Na-wat." The *l* in *tl* is only for the eyes), is what scholars call it, a word for their books. He called his language *Mexicano*, pronouncing it "Me-shi-ka-no."

A couple of little sugar skulls, *calaveras* left over from the previous days' festivities, grinned sweetly at me from over behind the glass display cases.

"My mother spoke beautiful Mexicano." His face softened. I found it hard to keep up with that face. The more I talked with him the more I felt he was a man of many moods, a man who had lived many lives. Now, smiling, his brown eyes shining, he looked fifty; now, frowning, his brow darkening as if shaded by an imaginary sombrero, he looked seventy. Frowning, he said, "I am not my mother. I mix my words." He meant that he used many Spanish words in his Mexicano sentences. It was a natural consequence of living in a country in which Spanish predominates.

Francisco explained that some Nahuas heap opprobrium on the practice. "They are few but they are very touchy about our language. Sometimes, if I say something like *hasta moztla*, you know, like *hasta mañana*, someone will say, 'Why are you talking to us in Spanish?' But that is just the way it is now. I'm too old to change. *Hasta moztla* feels natural to me. It is part of my language. Or I give someone the day of the week, and the person asking replies, 'Say it in Mexicano!' To which I say, 'Igual, it's the same, it's the same day in Spanish or in Mexicano.' And another thing. Let me tell you, the most extreme among them, they are funny. According to them, you shouldn't say you drive a *coche*. You should say you drive a *tepozyoyoli*. But no one says that. It means 'metal creature.' Imagine! 'I came here by metal creature.'"

And he let out a curt laugh.

Lockhart writes that some Aztecs went to similar lengths

to express in their own words what the Spaniards talked and gestured to them about. A dagger, for example, they tried calling *tepozteixilihuaniton* (literally, "little metal instrument for stabbing people"); *nequacehualhuiloni* ("thing for shading one's head") was their neologism for a hat. *Tlamelahuacachihualiztli* ("doing things straight") was what they came up with for the concept of law or justice. But none of these circumlocutions ever found many speakers — understandably enough. Like Francisco, most preferred to adopt — with minor tweaks — Spanish terms.

What mattered to the great majority of Nahuas was not the origin but the sound of a word. The word could come from more or less anywhere, Spanish, American English, Portuguese, you name it, provided that it sounded good. Francisco said, "When our mouths fall in love with a sound, we take it and speak with it." Nahuatl grammar was no object. The Nahuas' notion of a word was, it seems, far more subtle and inclusive than the Western one.

Reduplication, the repetition of a syllable within a word to alter or enhance its meaning, is the underpinning of the distinctive Mexicano sound. (Reduplication is rare in English. Something like it occurs in *reread* — a more consuming, emphatic action than reading is — or the much decried *pre-prepared*). *Kochi* means "sleep." Repeat the first syllable and you get *koh-kochi,* to be sound asleep. *Xotla* is to burn, *xoxotla,* to burn intensely. And these are only two from among the many dozens, scores, perhaps hundreds of possible examples the language offers.

It makes, as Francisco said, for a language that is most

welcoming to its environment's many shades of sound and nonhuman voices. A speaker can say *cocotl, cacalotl, papalotl* and instantly conjure up the white of a dove, the black of a crow, the fluttering of a butterfly, simply by naming each creature. Utter *huitzitzilin* and a hummingbird zips and thrums straight from your lips to the listener's imagination. It is why a Mexicano telephone does not merely "ring." To the Nahuas, its *tzitzilica* is reminiscent of the hummingbird's condensed, ear-catching frenzy. Rain here, too, is eloquent. A moderate shower, the kind that gradually empties markets and causes poplars to dribble, will *chichipica*; the same rain, turning white and fluffy in winter, will *pipixahui*. Indoors, on the stove, water heated in a pan starts to *huahualca* when it boils; corn cooked in a pan, on the other hand, is all *cuacualaca*. *Tzetzeloa* is another common household sound. It describes a shirt, a skirt, a blouse shaken out with any vigor.

And occasionally, to Mexicano ears, things can speak.

"My mother, she would say to me, 'You hear the clock? Listen to what the clock is telling you.' Always, work this and work that. That is what it was saying. Work. You have to work. *Tequiti* — it means 'to work.'"

Certain things, his mother would say, her son was not to pay any attention to. Strong gusts. Wells. Various types of bird. They had dirty mouths, she warned.

And once, Francisco remembered, his mother had told him about the words of lightning. Had he never noticed what lightning said?

I stopped him. *"Relámpago?"* I repeated the Spanish

word doubtfully. "Yes," he said, "*relámpago*, lightning." I waited for him to continue.

He took a glug of his coffee first.

"She told me that lightning says '*cuecueiuca*.'"

I thought, *yes, that is the sort of thing lightning would say*. Something bright and jagged. It was as if the lightning were, from what I could gather, narrating its own effect on the night sky. The word means "it is flaring" or "it is glinting."

The voice of lightning: *cuecueiuca!*

It is, I realized, an illustration of synesthesia. Lightning makes a deep impression on the viewer's optic nerve. The Mexicano mind sees a pattern, and in the pattern discerns a snap meaning. Sense and sound, in a flash of intuition, become complementary. Atmospheric electricity addresses the Nahua in labiovelars ($[k^w]$), and it simply feels right. Francisco said he couldn't explain any better why, to impersonate lightning, he had to round his lips.

A centuries-old culture, laden with an extraordinary sonic know-how, but it is on the wane. A reform of Mexico's constitution in 2003 granted Nahuas the belated right to education and government services in their language for the first time. But Francisco was worried. All around him, the evidence in his ears suggested ongoing decline. There are still more than a million up and down the country who speak Mexicano, but many resemble Francisco: men and women of a certain age. The young increasingly discard the language for fear of being thought *indios* by their Spanish-speaking compatriots and, unpersuaded by the arguments for bilingualism, disinherit the generations to come.

Outside the café, Francisco, full of coffee beans, whistled a bright little tune. He lived alone, he said. He missed talking. He didn't talk enough. Talking always did him a world of good.

The day after my conference—another warm, blue-sky day—I walked the streets of Puebla, all ears. The honks of passing cars. The sweet percussion of fountain water. Suddenly, not far from me, a squat pink church's bell began to toll. What did it say? I wondered. I would have liked to have had Francisco to ask.

Six

A CLOCKWORK LANGUAGE

Even in the biggest cities of Europe and North America, you can go a lifetime without hearing or seeing a word of the international auxiliary language Esperanto. No *saluton* ("hello"), no *dankon* ("thank you"). No *ne* ("no"). The scarcity of speakers has always put Esperantists at a disadvantage. The irony of their situation is plain. They are left defending the principle of a universal idiom in the very languages Esperanto was meant to supplant. So they talk up their literature in the language of Proust, Rimbaud, and Sartre; resort to German to remark how efficient and precise Esperanto is; proclaim its internationalism and exult in its flexibility—all in English. They sing the praises of its euphony in Italian. *Il faut lire Baghy! Sehr Logische! Speak the World's Language! Una lingua bellissima! Esperanto!* But their enthusiasm is not persuasive. It seems to suffer in translation. Difficult, then, for them to press their case with composure. Incomprehension is the least of their worries; what they really fear is indifference. Indifference tinged with mockery. Esperanto? Didn't that go out with the penny farthing? They are frequently mistaken for crackpots.

During the spring, summer, and autumn of 2015, I got to know several Esperantists. *Denaskaj Esperantistoj* (native Esperanto speakers), they had been brought up speaking the invented language from birth. The speakers' names and email addresses came courtesy of various groups to whom I had sent brief inquiries in my own (quite elementary) Esperanto — a vestige of my years as an adolescent swot. There was Peter, a sexagenarian teacher born in Aarhus to a German father and a Danish mother, who proved to be a diligent correspondent. Another was Stela, a twenty-something whose other mother tongue was Hungarian. A few more would reply sporadically, half-answer a couple of my questions, and volunteer the odd detail, only to vanish behind their pseudonyms.

They were Esperantists replying to messages written in Esperanto, but Peter and Stela initially employed a strange English that omitted grammar and made their sentences gappy and curt. It was as though they wanted to keep the language to themselves. Each, I realized, was sizing me up. Disappointed in the treatment they had received from the media, they were wary of anyone unaffiliated with the cause. My credentials needed parsing. Who was I exactly? What did I want? My Esperanto, such as it was, went a long way toward reassuring them. Before long, their reluctance yielded to eagerness; they were suddenly keen to talk to me, someone who saw them as much more than fodder for copy. And Stela remembered her boyfriend, a Frenchman, reading my first book, *Born on a Blue Day*. *La blua libro*, "the Blue Book," she called it.

Peter and Stela took me into their confidence. They switched to their mother tongue. I looked on their Esperanto sentences with something approaching astonishment. It fascinated me how the two of them thought and conversed so easily and naturally, just as if their words had evolved, accreted, from head to head, from mouth to mouth, over millennia. "To describe my Esperanto life is no easy task. So many experiences and memories. Which, among them, stand out? My mind resists. All my life the language has been a constant companion," Peter wrote (in my translation— my Esperanto improved rapidly during our correspondence). Similar passages appeared in Stela's emails. They reminded me of a twenty-year-old feeling—a thought until now unexpressed—produced by the library book in which I first read "iam estis eta knabo" ("once upon a time, a little boy"): this isn't some funny made-up lingo, but rather human language in one of its most recent and intriguing forms.

Ludwik Lejzer Zamenhof, who dreamed up Peter and Stela's mother tongue, was born in 1859 in the Polish city of Białystok, then a part of the Russian Empire. The son of a Jewish girls' tutor whose works included *A Textbook of the German Language for Russian Pupils,* young Ludwik grew up in a bookish, multilingual atmosphere. At home, he spoke Russian and Litvak Yiddish; at school, he acquired some French and German, conjugated Latin verbs, and deciphered texts in Greek. Polish, though frowned upon by the tsarist authorities, he picked up from some of his neighbors. And since God spoke Hebrew, the boy learned to read its characters from right to left and to say his prayers with a good accent. Yet, despite this studiousness, he could not always follow what was quoted, laughed at, gossiped over on a street corner, nor purchase the family's bread from just any market stall; on the contrary, in a city divided along language lines, it required nothing more than taking a wrong turn or mistaking one face for another for Ludwik to suddenly feel himself a foreigner in the eyes of a Belarusian seller, a Lithuanian loudmouth, a Ukrainian passerby.

Zamenhof knew from experience that in Białystok, a foreigner was often an object of suspicion and anger. There was the time his shortsighted eyes were drawn past a window to a group of long beards trudging up the wintry road that ran beside his parent's house. Suddenly, snowballs coming from all directions pelted the stunned men a powdery white; the thud, thud, thud in the boy's head was like gunshot. Through the windowpane he watched as the snowballs continued to fly. He made out the shouts of "Jewish swine!" that accompanied them, and his chest tightened. The shocked thought of the stones concealed within the snowballs made him wince. And when the throwers, out of ammunition, turned on their heels and fled, the boy heard them imitate the men's Yiddish in contemptuous snorts: "Hra — hre — hri — hro — hru."

"Hra — hre — hri — hro — hru." The sounds galvanized Zamenhof's imagination. A clever and high-strung student, he felt set apart, touched by specialness, and now he became obsessed with the dream of a unifying language that would make such taunts, and the prejudices behind them, disappear. It was the first stirrings of a lifelong labor.

Much of what we know about the beginnings of Esperanto comes from the early Esperantist Edmond Privat, whose readable 1920 Esperanto-language biography of Zamenhof — Peter in one of his emails had recommended it — slips only occasionally into hagiography. "Zamenhof had a head for outlandish ideas," Peter admitted. "The brotherhood of humanity, all that mystical stuff. Talking our way to world peace. Absurd! Of course, a shared language is no guarantee of mutual understanding. No panacea. Think of the former East and West Germany. Look at North and South Korea. Even we Esperantists are quick to quarrel. But he was on to something: an international language could at least carry ideas across seas, alleviate prejudice, broaden horizons. And he hit on just the right way to devise one that was both as simple as possible, and as complex as necessary, to put into words every human thought."

Zamenhof reached this "right way" through trial and error. He began by experimenting with a method first proposed by the Anglican clergyman John Wilkins in the seventeenth century and later written about in a little Borges essay: randomly assigning meanings to syllables. Each word arose from the steady concatenation of syllables and letters: the longer the word, the narrower the sense. Borges, in *The Analytical Language of John Wilkins,* informs us that *de* referred to an element in general; *deb,* "fire"; *deba,* "flame." *Zana,* "salmon," was a qualification of *zan,* "river fish," which itself qualified *za,* "any fish." In a similar "langue universelle," invented by Charles L. A. Letellier in 1850, *a* means "animal"; *ab,* "mammal"; *abo,* "carnivore"; *aboj,* "feline"; *aboje,* "cat." Zamenhof's own version of this scheme progressed no further than the sheets of school paper on which he jotted down line after line of unmemorable and barely distinguishable words.

Having failed at concocting an original vocabulary, Zamenhof busied himself with the idea of reviving his schoolmaster's Latin. He imagined populations once more orating as in the time of ancient Rome. But the language had those annoying declensions, which got his homework low marks; he would first have to simplify away all its endings, trim a noun like *domus* ("house") and its cohort of variants—*domuum, domōrum, domibus*—to a succinct *domo*. And then there were the cigars and the sugar cubes, the steam trains and the sewing machines, the bureaucrats and the rag-and-bone men for whom and for which no Latin word exists. The world had long since outgrown the Romans. And so, little by little, Zamenhof came to see his idea for what it was: another dead end. This realization, like his last, was a long time coming.

Finally, he settled on gleaning and blending words from all the languages that he heard at home, learned in school, or read in books. Each item of vocabulary would then be pressed into lexical molds of the teenager's devising—the nouns cookie cut into an *-o* ending, the adjectives into an *-a* ending, infinitives cut to end in *-i*—so that the resulting coinages possessed their own look and logic: *kolbaso* (from the Russian *колбаса* meaning "sausage"), *frua* (from the German *früh* meaning "early"), *legi* (from the Latin *legere* meaning "to read"). There remained, though, the danger that borrowing from many disparate sources might produce a linguistic mishmash. Zamenhof was missing a means to generate additional words from his coinages. The breakthrough came during one of his walks home from school, when a Cyrillic sign hanging outside a sweetshop snagged the student's attention. *Konditerskaya*, literally "a confectioner's place," bore a resemblance to the sign he'd once seen announcing a porter's lodge, *svejcarskaya* — literally, "a porter's place." The signs' resemblance, echoing the comparable function of the things they described, struck him as highly useful. Productive affixes like the Russian *-skaya* that marked various kinds of place, he realized, could give his nascent language further structure and help it cohere.

Words made out of such affixes dotted Peter's and Stela's messages. Esperanto contains a great many. In one email Peter wrote that he had been helping his *bofilino* ("daughter-in-law") move her things to a new address. A prefix, *bo-* (from the French *beau*, indicating a relation by marriage), and a feminizing suffix, *-ino* (*filo* means "son," *filino*, "daughter"), compose the noun. In another, he apologized for sending only a *mallonga* ("short") note. *Mal-* means "the opposite of." *Cerbumadi* ("to think about constantly"), an activity Stela indulges in — and a verb that I had never seen before — comprises *cerb-* ("brain"), *-um* (a suffix denoting a vague action), and *-adi* ("to do constantly"). Three composite words, and throughout my correspondents' pages there were dozens, scores, hundreds more.

Words that, in another country, another century, had been put together consciously, one by one by one, from scratch. To almost anyone else, the scale of such a task might have seemed impossibly discouraging. But once Zamenhof started, he found he could not stop. From time to time he must have paused to wonder whether he would ever tire of it, whether this mania would ever wear off, but that never happened. A schoolboy's hobby pushed to extreme lengths, the project consumed every minute of every hour of his free time. Day after week after month went into it. Alone though he was, the student was resourceful. He could be found flipping through the thickest dictionaries in the library, or compiling page after page of notes at his bedroom table, or asking his teacher unanswerable questions about which concepts might stick as well in a Malay's memory as in a Frenchman's. Every bout of progress in his tinkering, however small, however unstable, every newly conceived word or rule, gave him pleasure. *Anno,* his first pick for "year," he ultimately dropped in favor of *jaro,* swapping a Latin influence for a German—or perhaps Yiddish—one. His attempt at saying *and*—for a while *e*—turned to *kaj,* a rare Greek input, and made him shiver with delight. He was overjoyed to discover, single-mouthedly, that keeping the accent on a word's penultimate syllable helped with melody and ease of speech.

Mordechai Zamenhof did not share his son's enthusiasm. He hated the gibberish the boy came out with; he hated the many wasted hours diverted from studies—he had him down as a future doctor. Always on the edge of anger, he frowned and sighed and more than once gave Ludwik a stern talking-to. But Ludwik would not listen to reason. His refusal induced panic in his father. Would his eldest son shirk respectability for such a harebrained scheme?

Mordechai spoke to his son's schoolmaster. In his long service of children's education, he would have seen many a boyish eccentricity, many a hobby gone wrong. The schoolmaster confirmed the father's fears. The lad hadn't a sane nerve in his brain. Only madmen behaved likewise, wasting their lives on pointless pursuits. A serious scholar knew better than to mix and muddle languages. Soon rumors flew around the school that the Zamenhof boy was definitely cracked.

Ludwik could not stop—but for two years he had to. The hiatus was occasioned by his being sent away to Moscow to read medicine. In his absence, bales of notes—every trace of his years of solitary labor—went to cinders in his father's fireplace. Mordechai was determined not to have his family made into a laughingstock. But what he destroyed, Ludwik, on his return, restored word by word from memory. He packed his folders and bags for Warsaw, where he set up a modest ophthalmological practice, and became engaged to a soap manufacturer's daughter. At last he was free. He divided his time between eyeglasses-fitting, fiancée-squeezing, and putting the finishing touches to his "universala lingvo."

In ten years, Zamenhof's creation had gone from a few lines to a language, complete with nouns, pronouns, verbs, proverbs, adjectives, synonyms, rhymes. The only thing it was now lacking were speakers. So he drew up a forty-page pamphlet—a guide like the one his father had written for Jewish girls wanting to talk like Fräulein—and published it in 1887 under the title (in Cyrillic) *International Language. Foreword and Complete Textbook (for Russian Speakers)*. He was only twenty-eight. His nom de plume was Doktoro Esperanto ("Doctor Hoper").

Peter and Stela, to my surprise, had never looked at Zamenhof's pamphlet, the original Esperanto primer. Not that they did not read in Esperanto — Peter mentioned owning or having owned *La Grafo de Monte-Kristo,* a translation of Dumas' *The Count of Monte Cristo;* a short story collection, *La Bato (The Boat)*, by Lena Karpunina; early Esperanto novels, such as *Mr. Tot Aĉetas Mil Okulojn (Mr. Tot Buys a Thousand Eyes)*, by Jean Forge, and *Sur Sanga Tero (On Bloody Soil)*, by Julio Baghy; and the poet William Auld's epic *La Infana Raso (The Infant Race)*, among others. Stela had long ago read her Esperanto edition of *Winnie-the-Pooh* — *Winnie la Pu* — to pieces. But like most contemporary Esperantists, the two were unaware of the primer's contents and unmoved by its history. And indeed, when I read a digitized version of the pamphlet, I saw that it had hardly aged well. Its opening sentence — the first published in the language — is the stiff and baffling "Mi ne scias kie mi lasis la bastonon; ĉu vi ĝin ne vidis?" ("I do not know where I left the stick; have you not seen it?"). And then there is the odd tone throughout: earnest, touchy, glib. Zamenhof, full of his setbacks and frustrations, had infused the pamphlet's list of vocabulary with them: fighting words like *bati* ("to flog"), *batali* ("to fight"), *bruli* ("to burn"), *ĉagreni* ("to chagrin"), *detri* ("to destroy"), *disputi* ("to quarrel"), *insulti* ("to insult"), *militi* ("to struggle"), *ofendi* ("to wrong"), *puni* ("to punish"), *ŝanceli* ("to stagger"), *trompi* ("to deceive"), *turmenti* ("to torment"), *venki* ("to vanquish") abounded. A few years had sufficed to put many others out of date: *ekbruligu la kandelon* ("light the candle"), *kaleŝo* ("horse-drawn carriage"), *ŝtrumpo* ("stocking"), *telegrafe* ("telegraphically"), *lavistino* ("washerwoman").

But many saw the pamphlet differently at the time of its publication, having never seen anything of its like before. In the 1880s, voices the world over were crying out to be heard and understood. Geographic distance muffled them. Incomprehension among nations garbled them. So when the upper classes read the brand-new project in translation, they hailed "Doctor Hoper" as a pioneer on the level of Bell and Edison. The pamphlet made them utopian. Esperanto quickly became a household word among the wealthy. Within a year or two, thousands were relearning how to say their name (*mia nomo estas...*), ask questions (*Ĉu vi...?*), and count to ten: *unu, du, tri, kvar, kvin...*

Presently, letters addressed to the Doktoro in Warsaw started arriving. One correspondent complained that *"en mia urbo ĝis nun neniu ankoraŭ ion scias pri la lingvo Esperanto"* ("in my town to this day not one person knows anything about the Esperanto language"). Another wrote to ask whether it was correct to say *la malfeliĉo faris lin prudenta* ("misfortune made him prudent") or *la malfeliĉo faris lin prudentan* (Zamenhof replied "both"), and went on to sniff that *"la signetoj superleteraj estas maloportunaj en la skribado"* ("the superscript characters are inconvenient when writing"). But most of the letters were laudatory. A gentleman from Birkenhead, England, asked to receive more Esperantist publications, a request echoed in mail from Philadelphia and Paris. A novice in Kiev wrote a single line to commend the project as *tre interesa* ("very interesting"). A dentist in Saratov proposed a translation of Gogol. Zamenhof must have been delighted by the sight of his words in other hands. And not long after he began receiving the letters, he heard his creation spoken back to him. Antoni Grabowski was the speaker's name. He was a chemical engineer, turning thirty, who had Zamenhof's mustache and goatee and also his passion for languages. He had examined the pamphlet with the near-sighted attention he usually reserved for blueprints. He was smitten. He became an instant convert to Esperanto. He took a train to Warsaw, sought out the author's house, and knocked on the door. A thin, little, prematurely bald man opened. Zamenhof listened with dazzled pleasure to the stranger's stuttering yet familiar sentences and welcomed him inside. Alas for history, their exchange went unrecorded—neither man thought to commit it to paper; for the following reconstruction I have leaned on a near-contemporary textbook by Grabowski on conversational manners:

> "Ĉu vi estus Sinjoro Zamenhof?" ["Are you Mr. Zamenhof?"]
> "Jes!" ["Yes!"]
> "Sinjoro, mi havas la honoron deziri al vi bonan tagon."
>   ["Sir, I have the honor of wishing you good day."]

"Envenu, mi petas. Sidiĝu. Kiel vi fartas?" ["Come in, please. Take a seat. How are you?"]

"Tre bone, sinjoro, mi dankas. Kaj vi?" ["Very well, sir, thank you. And you?"]

"Mi fartas tre bone." ["I am very well."]

"Mi ĝojas vin renkonti." ["I am delighted to meet you."]

"Vi estas tre ĝentila." ["You are very kind."]

"Volu preni mian karton de vizito." ["Please take my business card."]

"Ĉu mi povas proponi al vi kafon aŭ teon?" ["May I offer you coffee or tea?"]

I can imagine Zamenhof saying something like this out of habit, without reflecting, since outside books, tea would still have been something of a rarity in those parts.

"Kafon." ["Coffee."]

"Ĉu vi deziras kremon?" ["Do you want cream?"]

"Ne, mi trinkas nur kafon nigran." ["No, I only drink black coffee."]

And after the niceties, the two men presumably got down to business. Probably they talked about the pamphlet, discussed ways to further the cause, or went over some of the finer points of Esperanto grammar. They would have refrained from straying into politics, let alone matters of the heart. The conversation would have talked itself out after half an hour or so.

The letters! The conversation over coffee! Fervently,

Zamenhof believed that his was an idea whose time had come. He pictured mouths by the thousand, million, rushing to pronounce his every sentence, foresaw the irresistible triumph of his utopia. He conceived it to be a revolution. Instead, it became merely a fashion. British publishers, angling for column inches, put out tiny print runs of *Teach Yourself Esperanto* phrasebooks. Continental hosts who wanted to impress their guests recited a few lines over wine and canapés. American dabblers in table-turning and simplified spelling switched fads. Every effort failed to turn these fair-weather speakers into dues-paying members. Most would not put their money where their mouths were. Most soon forgot the little they had once so enthusiastically learned. Months passed, years, and still no utopia. Zamenhof found himself with hardly a kopeck in his pocket; Esperanto had eaten all five thousand rubles of his wife's dowry.

His health was equally poor. He had to think about his heart. His heart was bad. People were surprised when he gave his age. Too much tobacco. Too little sleep. He had next to no appetite. He was always correcting some error-strewn letter, pulling together an exhorting sermon, thinking up another coinage. His life was one long language lesson.

Yet, increasingly, it must have seemed to Zamenhof that the teaching was being taken out of his hands. Ten years after his pamphlet, the center of the Esperanto-speaking world had moved westward to France. France became an economic lifeline: its intelligentsia subscribed many francs for the publication of periodicals. But the intellectuals also proposed to edit them as they saw fit. Strikingly ugly they thought the diacritics, those circumflexed *h*'s and *s*'s and the other supersigned characters, which continue to give today's keyboards hiccups; they wished to get rid of them. Zamenhof said he was willing to entertain the possibility. And there were other things the patrons wanted changed. They wanted the language to look more like Italian: don't say *du libroj* ("two books") but *du libri*. Again, Zamenhof said he could live with the idea. Adjectives, they added, should no longer have to agree with the nouns they described: don't say *grandaj libroj* ("big books") but *granda libri*. Nor, for that matter, should the object of a sentence require an *n*: not *mi legas grandan libron* ("I'm reading a big book") but *mi legas granda libro*. Zamenhof demurred. Dropping the diacritics and modifying words he could accept in principle; altering the way sentences worked, however, he could not.

The squabble continued on and off for years. In the end, the movement split into a mainstream of conservatives, led by Zamenhof, and a minority of reformers — tinkerers, to the conservatives — determined to do away with what they thought of as the creator's mistakes. The conservatives did away with them instead. Esperanto survived, but Zamenhof's optimism was shaken. In 1914, World War I broke out. Three years later, he died.

Peter: "One day, not long after the Great War, the village chimney sweep told my father all about an 'easy-to-learn international language.' My father had little schooling, but he could read, so he looked up and found an Esperanto course in the pages of the popular encyclopedia *Die Neue Volkshochschule*." The four-volume work also taught its readers stenography, graphology, hygiene, sport, and art, among other topics. "Later, he moved to the city, Hamburg, and became a policeman; he was active on the Esperanto scene there."

Weimar Germany, in the 1920s, was a land of strikes and uprisings, anger and hunger. The country was rife with anti-Semitic feeling. For German speakers of Esperanto, whose creator had been a Jewish Russo-Pole, it was a hard place to live. Racist slurs needed ignoring whenever they exchanged greetings in a busy street, shared news and anxieties, or gathered in someone's apartment or a public hall to commemorate Zamenhof's birthday. As early as 1926, Peter's father could have read in the national weekly *Der Reichswart* that Esperanto was a "freak of a language, without roots in the life of a people ... part of Zionist plans to dominate the world, and aid Zion's slaves to destroy the Fatherland." During a 1928 debate in the Bavarian state assembly about the possible introduction of Esperanto courses into German schools, the National Socialist deputy Rudolf Buttman put on record his contention that Esperanto was "a Jew's cobbled-together language, a thorn in the side of German culture." The National Socialists' own newspaper, the *Völkische Beobachter,* complained in 1930 that some Germans were "babbling" the language of "the bloodsucking internationalists."

Internationalist tendencies. It was for these that Peter's father was thrown out of the police force in 1932. Even among his fellow Esperantists he could find no refuge. Many, trying to accommodate themselves to the new regime, aping its bigotry, expelled "Jews, pacifists, profiteers" from their clubs. The clubs did not last long: in 1935 the National Socialist Minister Bernhard Rust closed them all down. Around the same time, a ban was enforced on letters written in either Esperanto or Hebrew. By then, Peter's father had fled for Holland, then for Norway, then for Denmark, where he taught beginning Esperanto for a living. "One of his students was my future mother. They married in 1937. After the German occupation, my father became an army chauffeur. He drove the military brass around and kept his head down. When the war started going wrong for the Nazis, he got called up, but he managed to wriggle out of it. His speaking Danish saved him: an interpreter was far more valuable to them than simply another pair of boots."

Peter was born in his mother's hometown in 1947. In the following year, his father moved back with his wife and son to Hamburg. In Hamburg, the father returned to his policeman's green uniform, his daily rounds, and his Esperanto club, where he taught evening classes. The family home was like a continuation of those classes: Peter would sit with Eliza, his kid sister, eating not Brot, Liverwurst, and Marmalade at the kitchen table but *pano, hepatokolbaso,* and *marmelado.* Brother and sister learned to speak their Esperanto with the father's earthy, *Plattdeutsch* accent. "His Esperanto skimped on any finery. No wonder, since my father hailed from a little burg inhospitable to education. His speech lacked the nuances of the well-schooled man." From their early childhood, Peter and his sister were regular clubgoers. He recalls smiling inwardly at the adults' blunders. "On rare occasions, I would even catch my father—a very active instructor—teach some point of grammar inaccurately (I didn't dare say anything)."

In one of his messages, Peter attached a color photograph of himself as a small, blond, rosy-cheeked boy. The boy is dressed in a tie and beige shorts, his white socks pulled right up to the knees. To his left, in the center, stands his father, rosy-cheeked and dark-suited, displaying proudly a child's drawing of the literary character Struwwelpeter. Behind Peter, a Christmas tree glitters. On the far left, his public: girls and women who sit or stand and beam. "I was five. I had had to learn by heart the story of Struwwelpeter in Esperanto." At his parents' club, he recited poems, sang songs, performed sketches. Sometimes foreign Esperantists came to visit. "If my memory serves me right, I spoke fluently with them—as fluently as any small child could."

Outside the home and club he was shyer. "Once, during a tram ride, my parents and I were talking together in Danish (my mother always spoke to me in her native tongue) when a Danish passenger joined in. I did not like the sound of him. I turned my back on the interrupter and carried on in Esperanto."

He began attending international Esperantist gatherings at the age of nine. "In 1956, I took part in the first Children's Congress. It was held in Denmark." Peter mixed with some thirty other children. One of the boys, about his age, had flown in from Texas. The Texan wore a cowboy suit, with a red sombrero on which someone had embroidered an eagle. The two started talking. "That we chatted in Esperanto seemed normal—in no way remarkable." The boys shared a group visit to the zoological garden in Copenhagen. "But all that time I could not take my mind off that hat!" After returning to Hamburg, Peter's parents took him as usual on their weekly visit to the club. "Turned out the boy's family had dropped in there on their way home to the States; they had left the cowboy hat there for me as a gift. I was very proud."

Before his teens he had never given a thought to the language. "For the first time I became aware of its rules. I began speaking more slowly, asking myself whether I had to cap this or that word with an -*n*." More and more, he found himself needled by grammatical scruples: should he say such-and-such sentence like this or like that? How could he know for certain whether what he was saying made complete sense? It was a phase he seems to have quickly grown out of. "I began to travel by myself. My confidence increased. I spent six weeks holidaying in Finland. I had no Finnish. My Danish and German were useless. And yet I never felt like a tourist. Unlike campers who have little contact with the country, I ate and slept in the homes of Finnish Esperantist families. My Esperanto was a passport to the world."

Peter has spent the greater part of his life traveling. "I have spoken Esperanto in Germany, Denmark, France, Finland, Sweden, the Netherlands, Poland, the Czech Republic, Slovakia, Slovenia, Croatia, Serbia, Bosnia and Herzegovina, Austria, Australia, Britain, Spain, China, Nepal, Iceland, and the United States." In Croatia, he met his first wife. "It was during an Esperantist seminar. She spoke no German, and I no Croatian." Her Esperanto charmed him. "The Serbs and Croats are the best pronouncers." They whispered sweet nothings, gossiped with each other, disputed memories, all in the language. Their marriage was childless; Peter later adopted a boy and a girl. "My son lives only for football. As for my daughter, she was already an adult; I only managed to teach her a smattering of words. I suppose, from the movement's viewpoint, I haven't been a very successful Esperanto parent."

His sister has had more success. He told me, "My niece and nephew are both native speakers. But, from what I can gather, the boy has let his Esperanto go. My niece married a native speaker but they aren't active in the movement." He and his sister are no longer on speaking terms.

In all our exchanges Peter struck me as a man who lived for the cause. He had written many polite, rectifying letters to the papers. "For many years I subscribed to *Die Zeit,* and would write in from time to time about Esperanto. An editor finally replied to inform me that the paper's policy forbade him to publish anything positive about the language. Times change, though, and gradually mention of Esperanto is creeping back into print." He was not, he insisted, a proselytizer. "I don't conceal my convictions. I often wear a lapel pin showing the movement's green flag. But I don't go in for preaching."

At fifty, he decided to return to his birthplace; he now lives an hour's drive from Copenhagen. "I can go for days without speaking a word of Esperanto. The nearest club is in the capital, and I only rarely venture over. The language is more for the telephone, and the computer." He splits his life between his three native tongues. "I do all my sums in German. How I jot down a grocery list depends on where I shop: here in Denmark, I use Danish. When I visit Germany, German. A note reminding me to buy such-and-such Esperanto book I make in Esperanto." And some nights, he dreams in Esperanto. "They seem to crop up after I've spent several days at one of the various get-togethers."

Does he believe the language has a future? "I hope so. It's like a legacy passed down through the generations."

Stela, a sociologist in her twenties, is part of the new generation of native speakers. Stela is her Esperanto name. Hungarians call her Eszter. Her father was a French school-teacher; her mother, a Budapest-based commercial translator. Both were dedicated Esperantists. Her father, though, had another life back in France. "He only visited my mother and me from time to time. You might say he was a character. His Esperanto was good, not perfect; he was always dropping his *n*'s." Stela's came from her mother, who learned to speak it faultlessly at university.

Stela, unlike Peter, remembers her first word. "My mother was pushing me somewhere in the buggy when I saw an oncoming tram, raised my index finger, and shouted *Vidu!* ('Look!')." Hungarian she learned to speak at school. "I never understood why my classmates thought my speaking Esperanto with my mother was so curious. Some of the other children spoke foreign languages at home: Russian, for example, or German." At times she had trouble telling her two languages apart: "I would get my words mixed up. I would say *pampelegér* for 'grapefruit': a combination of the Esperanto *pampelmuso* and the Hungarian *egér*."

Her bookish mother's daughter, Stela read and read and read. Her bedroom shelves were crammed with colorful Esperanto books. One of her favorite titles, she told me, had been *Kumeŭaŭa, la filo de la ĝangalo (Kumewawa, the Son of the Jungle)*, by the Hungarian Esperantist author Tibor Sekelj. She told me this quite offhandedly, without preliminaries, as though the story were a classic. And, when I googled for more details, I discovered to my astonishment that it was. A children's adventure yarn, first published in 1979, and many times translated, it has enjoyed a long career throughout the globe's bookshops. In Tokyo it was apparently once as big as *The Little Prince*. I managed to track down the original summary:

> On the river Aragvajo, an affluent of the Amazon, a group of tourists is in danger. Their ship has sunk. A good thing Kumewawa steps forward to help them. "Fish we measure according to their length; men, according to their knowledge." Kumewawa is only twelve years old, but belongs to the Karajxa tribe and knows everything there is to know about life in the jungle.

But despite Kumewawa's escapades, the sinking ships and the daring rescues, Stela, like many of her generation, slowly lost interest in reading. "I wouldn't recognize one of Zamenhof's proverbs or expressions. I don't have that culture. Some learners might, but for me the culture resides in my family and friends." Curiously, her mother ceased using the language with her once she turned twenty. "She simply said to me: 'I've taught you all I know.' Before then the only time she spoke to me in Hungarian was when she lost her temper." It is to her friends in the movement, her second family, that she feels closest. "Growing up, I failed to understand why the other Hungarians considered their summer holidays as purely family time. I always spent my summers overseas with other Esperantists."

Both Peter and Stela wrote warmly of the movement's various international meetings: in clubs, congresses, and other get-togethers. It was clear, from their differing accounts, that the meetings had varied over the years. In Peter's day, they had been formal, requiring ties and good manners. Today, bare feet and bottles of plonk are everywhere to be seen. Peter's generation had organized sparkly balls. Stela's slaps tables with playing cards. Peter confided that the food, which students prepared for the attendees, was consistently bad: all grease and wilting vegetables; probably the badness of the food is one of the few things that hasn't changed.

Certainly, Esperanto has changed. Its evolution is one of the things that animated Peter and Stela most. The evolution betokens an adaptive, natural-like language. Some changes, the smallest, have been motivated by technological advances: Peter long ago stopped saying *kasedaparato* ("cassette player"); the same sounds, with few alterations, he recycles these days to talk about the *kafaparato* ("coffee machine"). Text messaging has abbreviated the most common words: Stela texts *k* for *kaj* ("and"), *bv* for *bonvolu* ("please"), *cx* for *ĉirkaŭ* ("about"). Other modifications are cultural, born out of a youngster's desire not to sound like Granny and Gramps. For Peter, something excellent is simply *bonega* (literally "greatly good"), whereas for Stela it is *mojosa* ("cool"). "I was at the teen meetup where it was first spoken," Stela told me. The new word caught on fast. "Now at every youth event it's mojosa this and mojosa that."

The biggest and least reported shifts have been internal. Shades of meaning have progressively changed words. A hundred years ago, owing to the influence of Russian, boats and ships *naĝis* ("swam"); nowadays, they sail. The example is Jouko Lindstedt's, an Esperantist linguist. Another such case concerns the word *versaĵo* (literally "a piece of verse"), which has long since been supplanted by *poemo,* a term that originally referred only to the epics. Also, the way words link up to convey more complex meanings has altered over the past hundred years, the phrases becoming progressively shorter. Zamenhof would have said something like *ĝi estus estinta ebla* ("it would have been possible"); Peter, to express the same thing, says *ĝi estus eblinta;* Stela says, *ĝi eblintus.* And with this evolution, the idea of a good Esperanto sentence — one that feels more Esperanto than another — has gradually emerged. Claude Piron — an influential figure in the movement — discouraged a sentence like *en tiu epoko li praktikis sporton kun vigleco* ("at that time he practiced sport with vigor") in favor of the swifter *tiuepoke li vigle sportis* (literally "that-time-ly he vigorously sport-ed").

Swifter, perhaps, but Piron's sentence, like most in the

language, remains confined to paper or a computer screen. Esperanto has always been an overwhelmingly written language. "Quite often, I require a few minutes to get into my normal flow when I speak Esperanto," Stela admitted. "I'm forever writing in it, but speaking and writing aren't the same thing." That is why the congresses were so important to her and Peter. They provided momentary spaces in which to converse, but such conversations could hardly be altogether satisfying. Or natural. Many of the attendees were eternal beginners, forever glancing down at their notes as if standing at a podium. Misunderstanding was only ever a fluffed vowel away.

It is one thing to flex syntax. It is another thing to understand what is being said or written. Ken Miner, another Esperantist linguist, has written several papers — in Esperanto — in which he highlights ambiguities. Does the simple-looking sentence *mi iris en la ĝardenon* mean "I went into the garden" or "I was on my way into the garden"? Peter, when I asked him, thought the former, but Miner said quite a few other speakers, even the most experienced, disagree. In another paper, Miner discusses the suffix *-ad*. Textbooks tell learners that it indicates duration: *kuri* ("to run"), *kuradi* ("to run and run"). But Miner, burrowing into Esperanto literature, found plenty of sentences that contradicted the rule: *li atendadis dum horoj* ("he waited and waited for hours") but *pacientoj atendas dum monatoj* ("patients wait for months"), where the first uses *-ad* to describe a wait lasting hours, but not the second for one that goes on and on for months.

These ambiguities and inconsistencies, explains Miner, are the result of non-natives having shaped Esperanto. Without a native speaker's intuitions, Zamenhof and his first followers had had no choice but to rely on logic; languages, however, by their nature, are often illogical. The users' judgments, each under the sway of their respective grammars (Polish, Russian, English, French...), had clashed. To this day, they still do. Not even Peter and Stela can tell for sure whether certain sentences are right or wrong. Their intuitions, forged in a non-Esperanto-speaking society, are unreliable. Peter, at various points, told me as much. "Don't think that native Esperanto speakers automatically speak flawlessly! There exist notable counterexamples." Much depends on the parents' degree of fluency. Some touted as natives, it turns out, speak only a kitchen Esperanto.

Miner's research, Peter's remarks: they came as something of a surprise. They ran counter to the confidence with which the movement promotes its "easy-to-learn" language. Peter, though, was unsurprised by my surprise: "About the average level among learners, I can only speak from experience. Most have little grasp of the language. Esperanto isn't as easy as some of our adepts like to affirm." Quirks and contradictions, no different from those that learners of any language encounter, are to blame. The *Plena Manlibro de Esperanta Gramatiko* (the complete handbook of Esperanto grammar) spans some seven hundred pages. And when I looked again at the assertions the movement had published — "For a native English speaker, we may estimate that Esperanto is about five times as easy to learn as Spanish or French, ten times as easy to learn as Russian, twenty times as easy to learn as Arabic or spoken Chinese, and infinitely easier to learn than Japanese"—I felt that they were only salesman words, salesman numbers, without foundation.

One hundred and thirty years ago, Zamenhof's stated goal had been ten million speakers—ten million to start with. When asked by an Associated Press reporter in 1983 to estimate the global number of speakers, the movement's president, Grégoire Maertens, replied, "I usually say 10 million people read and understand Esperanto. Speaking is another thing. But then, how many people speak their own language correctly?" I believe this is wishful thinking. I cannot take seriously the claims made in the papers, that more speak Esperanto than speak Welsh or Icelandic; that it is on a par with Hebrew and Lithuanian. And none of the promoters seem to have taken into account population inflation: ten million in 1887 would be fifty million in 2017. No article, though, has printed a figure of fifty million, not even in the most enthusiastic columns of the Esperantist press. In linguistics circles, the actual figure of active, competent Esperanto speakers is estimated much, much lower. Ken Miner and his colleagues put it at fifty thousand. Fifty thousand, give or take, is the number who speak the Greenlandic Kalaallisut.

Humans everywhere use language, but only rarely choose which. Each is some person's birthright. Peter and Stela were born into Esperanto, two of probably no more than a thousand such speakers. So why have the others, several tens of thousands, volunteered to master it? Not for any practical purpose: English, natural to hundreds of millions, has become the world's primary medium of communication. Nor is it because Esperanto learns itself: It is as complex and capricious as any other language. Deeper needs—to stand out or apart, to flatter the conscience, to integrate into a tight-knit community—lie behind the learner's decision. Esperanto simplifies the world, neatly divides it into two: on one side, all the men and women in the dark, those who have stopped up their ears, the trucklers to the powers-that-be; on the other, those who can truthfully say "Mi parolas Esperanton."

A comforting abstraction, but Peter, at least, is old enough to know better. Once, during our many exchanges, I broached the subject of favorite words. I had unearthed a survey conducted among Esperantist writers, poets, and other personalities, and sent it to him. I thought it a way to get him talking about Esperanto's emotional charge. I was wrong. Peter wrote back that words, by themselves, in whatever language, could never do justice to the world. It was what Stela had meant when she explained that her culture resided in her family and friends. "These sorts of lists leave me cold," he wrote. "Why should *mielo* ["honey"] be considered a more beautiful word than *marmelado?* I have never seen or heard a *najtingalo* sing. But two winters ago, here in the Danish countryside, not far from my home, I taught a wild pheasant to eat out of my hand. For me, *fazano* has a much finer ring than *najtingalo.*"

Seven

THE MAN WHO WAS FRIDAY

N gũgĩ wa Thiong'o, the Grand Old Man of African letters, is telling me how he wrote *Caitaani mũtharaba-Inĩ* (*Devil on the Cross*), the first Kikuyu-language novel, on prison toilet paper.

When did it all begin? The midnight before New Year's Eve, 1977. I was with my family in Limuru when armed policemen came and shoved me into a Land Rover. It was an abduction: there was no reason in law to drive me away. Next day, Saturday, they put me in chains. They took me to Nairobi, to the Kamiti Maximum Security Prison. I lost my name, Ngũgĩ. The prison officers called me only by the number on my file: K677. We, the other detainees and I, were considered political dissidents by the Kenyatta regime. For one year I was held without trial. My daughter Wamuingi was born in my absence. I received the news in a letter with a photograph enclosed. The first weeks were the hardest. I felt very lonely. But the other prisoners knew me and my work. They were encouraging.

Some of them had books they lent me to read. Dickens. Aristotle. Some gave me biros and pencils as gifts. And there was another source of motivation to write. One day a warder complained to me that we educated Kenyans were guilty of looking down on our national languages. I could not believe my ears! That night I sat at my desk in my cell and let the beginning of a story in Kikuyu pour out of me. For paper, of course, I had only that provided in bundles by the authorities to meet a prisoner's bodily needs. The toilet paper was thick and rough, and intended to be rough, but what was bad for the body was good for the pen. The bigger problem was the language. My Kikuyu looked funny on paper. I had no experience of writing at such length in Kikuyu. Once again, my friends in the prison were very kind, very helpful. They helped me to find the right word for this scene or that character. They taught me songs and proverbs I hadn't heard before. I wrote the story's final sentences only days before learning that I was to be released. The book was published in Nairobi two years later, in 1980.

Having bared his prison story to me, its trauma and its triumph, he smiles, looking younger than his seventy-seven years, and returns to his plate of *foie gras poêlé avec tartare de légumes*. We are talking over lunch in the French coastal town of Nantes. May in Nantes is already summery. We are on the busy terrace of a restaurant a short walk from Ngũgĩ's hotel. Below the terrace, literary festivalgoers, between events, traipse or cycle along the canal; a few look up when Ngũgĩ stands abruptly and steps out of the parasols' shade to the railing to take a call. His black shirt is embroidered with a bright golden-elephants design; his baggy, beige slacks finish in a pair of black, worn-out trainers. His Kikuyu (the indigenous language of over six million Kenyans) — fast and loud and emphatic — so unlike his English of the previous minutes, so unlike the French of the surrounding tables, fills the air. Nantes, as the town's statues and street names remind us, is the birthplace of Jules Verne. Is Ngũgĩ, to the festivalgoers on foot or bike who steal looks as they pass, "Africa"? Verne's Africa?

> Immense brambly palisades, impenetrable hedges of thorny jungle, separated the clearings dotted with numerous villages....Animals with huge humps were feeding in the luxuriant prairies, and were half hidden, sometimes, in the tall grass; spreading forests in bloom redolent of spicy perfumes presented themselves to the gaze like immense bouquets; but, in these bouquets, lions, leopards, hyenas and tigers, were crouching for shelter from the last hot rays of the setting sun. From time to time an elephant made the tall tops of the undergrowth sway to and fro, and you could hear the crackling of huge branches as his ponderous ivory tusks broke them in his way. (From *Five Weeks in a Balloon*.)

Ngũgĩ is on his way to Kenya. (Nantes, for its international writers' festival, is a brief stopover.) He has lived in exile in the West, mostly in the United States, where he has taught comparative literature at the University of California, Irvine, since 1982. Trips to his homeland are few and far between, and this one—his first in over ten years—might be his last. So it is a piece of luck, his coming here (a two-hour train ride from Paris), and my learning of it in time; and it is generous, or indulgent, of him to agree to meet with me to talk language and language politics when he must have many things on his mind.

In much of Kenya, where English, alongside Kiswahili, is the official language, his politics are controversial. Ngũgĩ has long argued that African authors should write and publish in African languages ("Why should Danish, with five million people, be able to sustain a literature but not the Yoruba, who are forty million?"); that African intellectuals should reason and debate in African languages. English, he insists, is not an African language. It is an argument that has set him apart from many of his contemporaries. The Yoruba author Wole Soyinka wrote his plays and poems in English; Chinua Achebe, an Igbo, wrote his novels and essays in English. In his 1965 essay "The African Writer and the English Language," Achebe pointed out that his was "a new English, still in full communion with its ancestral home but altered to suit its new African surroundings." An Igbo English. But for Ngũgĩ, such defenses fail to hold up. Soyinka and Achebe, he thinks, write as Africans estranged from their languages by the legacy of European colonialism. They write as white-cloaked surgeons whose African characters speak with transplanted tongues.

Consciousness of language politics came early to Ngũgĩ. In 1952, when thousands of the dispossessed Kikuyu began rising up against the colonial administration, he was a schoolboy of fourteen. The violent revolt by Kenya's largest ethnic group panicked the British into declaring a state of emergency. All nationalist-run school administrations across the land were fired and replaced with ones sympathetic to the Crown. The sudden changes deprived Ngũgĩ and the other rural children — pickers of tea leaves — of their indigenous-language curricula. Instead of traditional songs, the pupils read *Robinson Crusoe;* instead of tales learned around a village fire, Shakespeare. Ngũgĩ, whose Kikuyu compositions had once been his teacher's pride, saw his classmates punished for speaking the language. They were struck with a cane or made to wear metal plates around their necks bearing the words "I am stupid" or "I am a donkey." Lucky, resolute, he himself was never a donkey. To his surprise and relief he took at once to the English books. English, in his skillful hands, would bring him various student prizes and, in 1964, to Britain on a scholarship to study at the University of Leeds.

I don't tell Ngũgĩ, when he returns from his call, my admiration for his first novels: *Weep Not, Child, The River Between,* and *A Grain of Wheat,* a trio originally published in London in the 1960s by the Heinemann African Writers Series. I don't tell him how the deceptively simple, evocative opening to *The River Between* gets me every time, a pleasure that no amount of rereading seems to dim.

The two ridges lay side by side. One was Kameno, the other was Makuyu. Between them was a valley. It was called the valley of life. Behind Kameno and Makuyu were many more valleys and ridges, lying without any discernible plan. They were like many sleeping lions which never woke. They just slept, the big deep sleep of their Creator.

I don't tell him, because Ngũgĩ would later call these works — which he wrote in English and published under his childhood name of James Ngũgĩ during his years in Leeds — his "Afro-Saxon novels," the better to distance himself from what he considers to be their relative inauthenticity compared with his subsequent writings in Kikuyu. To write in Kikuyu while imprisoned was, for him, an act of autonomy, of self-determination. More than sounds and stories linking him to his formative years, the language, in Ngũgĩ's mind, became a repudiation of the country's English-speaking elite. The gesture was brave (he was always having to squirrel the toilet paper manuscript away from guards); it was eloquent. And yet, something in Ngũgĩ's disregard for his earlier work, his argument about English in Africa rankles with me. I voice my thoughts.

"You wrote your first, *the* first, novel in Kikuyu in the 1970s. But hasn't the relationship between Africa and the English language continued to change since then? What about the rise of post-independence Africans who feel completely comfortable in their English, authors like Chimamanda Ngozi Adichie and Chris Abani?"

(I mention Abani for a reason. We once met at a writers' event in the United States and discussed the "language question." Abani grew up in Nigeria. His father is Igbo. His mother is British. So English, in which Abani writes, is for him a native language. And it was for writing, in English, what were construed as dissident texts by the English-speaking Nigerian government, that he was put behind bars at the age of eighteen and then on death row. His release two years later was like a rebirth. But he never thought about writing in Igbo; it would have felt inauthentic, he said.)

Ngũgĩ says, "These authors have an inheritance. They should contribute to it. They have a duty to protect it."

And, listening between the lines, I think I understand the two ideas of inheritance that Ngũgĩ's word contains. The first, postcolonial, says African authors must take up pens to show that *third world* doesn't mean "third-rate," that African languages are the equals of their European counterparts: equally rich and complex and artful. The second, ancestral, says language is a natural resource of collective memory: a unique way of being in and knowing the world.

"There's now a whole generation of young people in Africa who, through no fault of their own, do not speak their African mother tongue. You might say, 'English or French is their mother tongue.' No. English isn't African. French isn't African. It isn't their fault, but that's how it is. What would I say to a native English-speaking African? If you are born in an English-speaking household, there's no reason for you not to learn an African language at school. Kiswahili. Kikuyu.

Igbo. Yoruba. Whatever. And then use your English to translate works into African languages."

There is nativist rhetoric in Ngũgĩ's references to "African mother tongues" and "African languages." It reminded me, a little uncomfortably, of things I had heard in Britain about the decisions of several councils, with their large immigrant communities, to erect road and street signs in other orthographies: Polish, Punjabi. Those opposed to the signs had declared that neither Polish nor Punjabi was a British language. That, too, was intended to pass for an argument. But terms such as "African languages," like "British languages," make little, if any, sense, linguistically speaking. They are proxies for personal opinions, depending entirely for their meaning on whom you ask. I suppose every African draws the line somewhere, and Ngũgĩ draws it at English and French. Fair enough. But then, Ngũgĩ's position, I learned, is less personal than it is ideological, with the incongruities that ideology brings. For example, does he consider Kiswahili—a widely spoken Bantu lingua franca composed of many Arabic, Persian, and Portuguese influences—African?

"Yes."

"Arabic?" Language of the continent's first colonizers, ivory and slave traders.

"Yes."

"Afrikaans?"

He hesitates. "Yes."

I try to get him to divulge his reasoning, but it isn't easy. He only says, by way of explanation, that many poor black children in South Africa speak Afrikaans. I do not press him. Already his knife and fork hover over the remains of the foie gras.

Ngũgĩ's thinking can be traced back to the mid- to late 1960s, his postgraduate student days in Leeds: the heady mix of Marx and Black Power. *Lumpenproletariat! Black Skin, White Masks!* No longer would he be the young author who could write, in a 1962 opinion piece for Kenya's *Sunday Nation,* "I am now tired of the talk about 'African culture': I am tired of the talk about 'African Socialism.'... Be it far from me to go about looking for an 'Africanness' in everything before I can value it." That was before Leeds. Now, on his return to Nairobi, a thirty-year-old professor at the capital's university, he proposed to abolish the English department in favor of a department of African literature and languages. He renounced his schoolboy Protestantism, and with it the name *James,* of his first books. His writing grew darker, more didactic.

In his 1985 essay *On Writing in Kikuyu,* Ngũgĩ describes the precursor to his imprisonment: the six months he spent in 1977 working with the villagers of Kamiriithu to stage the play *Ngaahika Ndeenda ("I Shall Marry When I Want"),* about greedy imperialists who exploit brave Kikuyu peasants. In keeping with his collectivist thinking, he intended the project to be a group effort. The men and women of the village were duly quick to correct his numerous Kikuyu mistakes: "You university people, what kind of learning have you had?"

"I learnt my language anew," Ngũgĩ concedes. But he was

proud, with much to feel proud about: The participatory theater project did a lot of good. Some of the villagers learned to read and write. Others, feeling valued, having something for their minds to do, drank less, so that alcoholism, the scourge of many Kenyan villages, was alleviated. Several discovered in themselves an actor's bravado or other talents that might otherwise have stayed forever dormant. The popular enthusiasm was such that the play's rehearsals immediately drew large crowds. Hundreds, then thousands, from the surrounding villages came and sat in the open air — and listened, shouted, clapped, laughed, booed. It was enough to make the authorities jumpy. Ngũgĩ became a man with enemies in high places.

The play was hastily banned; the village theater group disbanded, its grounds razed. And on the night of December 30, 1977, armed policemen with an arrest warrant rode past maize fields, tethered goats, and chicken coops to the only house in Limuru with a telephone wire.

Hoping, by incarcerating Ngũgĩ's voice, to silence him, the regime unwittingly made him a cause célèbre. In London, members of the Pan African Association of Writers and Journalists massed before the Kenyan embassy and held up placards that read "Free Ngũgĩ." A letter to the editors in the June 1978 issue of the *New York Review of Books* urged governments to push for the author's release; its signatories included James Baldwin, Margaret Drabble, Harold Pinter, Philip Roth, and C. P. Snow.

It is surprising, then, that after his liberation Ngũgĩ was allowed to publish his novel. Perhaps the regime intended to placate the international uproar the author's imprisonment had provoked. Perhaps, the Kikuyu was simply too much work for censors used only to reading in English and Kiswahili. Perhaps, going only on the book's original cover, a cartoonish drawing that showed a paunchy white man hanging from a dollar-studded cross, the regime thought the book nothing more than an anti-imperialist tract. (Indeed, the title, *Caitaani mũtharaba-inĩ*, can be understood as "The Great Satan on the Cross.")

Whatever its reason for allowing the novel's release, the regime underestimated the Kikuyus' appetite for a publication in their own language. The story of a young village woman who confronts the seedy foreign-money corruption in her country proved popular. In his essay, Ngũgĩ relates how the book was read aloud by literate members of a family to their neighbors, all ears. In bars, he writes, a man would read the choicest pages to his fellow drinkers until his mouth or glass ran dry—at which point a listener would rush to offer him another beer in return for the cliffhanger's resolution.

Like most of Ngũgĩ's international audience, I don't know Kikuyu and had to content myself with the author's own English translation of the story. (Other translations have appeared in Kiswahili, German, Swedish—and Telugu, in a version created by the activist poet Varavara Rao during his own prison stint.) So I ask him now if he could teach me a few Kikuyu words from the book. He sees me readying my pen and notepad, and—so promptly and proprietorially that I'm taken aback—he reaches over and lifts them from my hands. He says, as my pen in his hand writes, "*kana,* infant." It could also mean "fourth" or "to deny" or "if" or "or," depending on how you say it. *Turungi,* he says, is a very Kikuyu word. "It means 'tea.'" *Kabiaru,* another "very Kikuyu word," is "coffee." In Kenya, home of tea leaves and coffee beans, I can easily see how these words might have associations — social, cultural — that are particular to the Kikuyu imagination. But even if they do, both, as Ngũgĩ goes on to explain, happen to be English imports: *turungi,* from "true tea" and "strong tea"; *kabiaru* from "coffee alone," meaning black, no milk.

(And, later, with the help of Kikuyu scholars, I will discover just how much vocabulary Ngũgĩ's Kikuyu works — plays, novels, children's stories — owe to English: *pawa* ["power"], *hithituri* ["history"], *thayathi* ["science"], *baní* ["funny"], *ngirini* ["green"], *túimanjini* ["let's imagine"], *athimairíte* ["while smiling"], *riyunioni ya bamiri* ["family reunion"], *bathi thibeco* ["special pass"], *manínja wa bengi* ["bank manager"]. It also turns out that the extent of this borrowing is quite vexing to some Kikuyu critics. Why, for example, does Ngũgĩ write *handimbagi* ["handbag"] when Kikuyu has its own word, *kamuhuko?* Why does he write *ngiree* ["gray"] when Kikuyu already has *kibuu?*)

English has fed Kikuyu (as French long fed English, as Arabic fed Kiswahili). It is why history is too complex, too many-sided, it seems to me, for the binary readings — African versus European, indigenous versus imperialist, black versus white, poor versus rich — of much language politics. In the person of the Victorian settler, the British expelled many Kikuyu from their land and homes; in the person of the colonial policeman, they shouted and shot at African protesters demanding equal rights. Many colonizers committed atrocities. Nothing can justify the baseless stupidity of the colonialist worldview. But even in the grubbiest circumstances, men and women of all tongues can perform small acts of humanity. English was also the language in which the Kenyan-born paleontologist L. S. B. Leake—a fluent Kikuyu speaker—compiled his magnum opus *The Southern Kikuyu Before 1903*. Running some 1,400 pages, it is a paean to the social, cultural, and linguistic riches of the Kikuyu people. One section lists the traditional names of over four hundred species of plant; another gives the precise lexicon to describe the various colors and markings on goats, cattle, and sheep. In the person of the liberal Anglican, English devised Kikuyu's orthography, published Kikuyu dictionaries and grammars, built schools. For all its paternalism, the language doubled as the language of African aspiration. When, in the 1920s, educators proposed dropping English in favor of teaching in Kikuyu, Luhya, or Luo, many parents recoiled; English, they understood, was a potential leveler, a gateway to the wider world.

Ngũgĩ's own children, several of them writers, have this idea of English. I learn this toward the end of our conversation, when the young server comes for our plates. I am asking Ngũgĩ what his offspring think of his ideas; in place of speaking, he picks up my pen and notepad again and writes. Beside the names of his sons and daughters appear the titles of their respective books: *Nairobi Heat, The Fall of Saints,*

City Murders, Of Love and Despair. All English. His son Mūkoma, the author of *Nairobi Heat,* is presently an assistant professor in the English department at Cornell. Is his father disappointed?

He isn't. Or so he says. He shrugs. Children will be children.

But even were his children to ever start writing in Kikuyu—as Francophone authors Pius Ngandu Nkashama of the Congo, and Boubacar Boris Diop of Senegal also write in Tshiluba and Wolof, respectively—other obstacles, cultural, technological, economic, remain. In indigenous languages no author can yet aspire to scrape much of a living. According to a report by the Kenya news agency, dated July 30, 2014,

> In developing countries like Kenya, there is a serious lack of reading materials.... In Kiambu County... there are no public libraries where people can quench their reading thirst, and this has seemingly led to poor reading culture within the area.... In USA, a child is introduced to a library at as early age as five years, unlike in Africa where even university students are not acquainted to or are "allergic" to libraries.

Another agency item, put out a few weeks before my meeting with Ngũgĩ, carried the stark headline "Few Customers in Bookshops."

Ngũgĩ remains cautiously optimistic about the future of Kikuyu and other African-language literature. He has reasons to hope. One is the annual Mabati-Cornell Kiswahili

Prize for African Literature, co-founded in 2014 by Ngũgĩ's son, Mũkoma, which awards original writing in Kiswahili. The bigger one, by far, is translation. In February 2015, the Nigerian publisher Cassava Republic brought out *Valentine's Day Anthology,* a downloadable collection of short romance stories by leading African authors. Each story had been translated from English into an indigenous language such as Kpelle, Kiswahili, Yoruba, Igbo, or Hausa. And Cassava Republic is not alone. Ceytu, a new imprint in Senegal, recently translated *The African,* a novel by the French-Mauritian Nobel laureate J. M. G. Le Clézio, into Wolof.

Colleagues wait for Ngũgĩ at his hotel. Before taking my leave, I ask him if he could teach me one more Kikuyu word, the one word that everyone ought to know. In my notepad he writes, in the same firm, elegant hand as, forty years earlier, he wrote on prison toilet paper: *thayũ.*

Peace.

Eight

ICELANDIC NAMES

Jóhannes Bjarni Sigtryggsson has to decide whether or not *Cleopatra* is Icelandic. It is, he knows, a decision which cannot be taken lightly: in the balance lies the future self-image of a couple's newborn daughter. It is, furthermore, a decision which Jóhannes doesn't take alone. He shares the little room in the capital's three-story National Registry building with a senior lecturer in law and another academic working in Icelandic studies. The three, meeting monthly, compose Iceland's *Mannanafnanefnd,* the Persons' Names Committee, charged with preserving the nation's ancient infant-naming traditions. Every month, sometimes six, sometimes eight, sometimes ten submissions from parents or prospective parents (along with checks in the amount of 3,000 krónur, about 25 dollars) reach the committee. On average, between one-half and two-thirds of the names proposed will be approved by the members and duly entered in the register, which presently counts 1,888 boys' names and 1,991 girls'. The task is endless: parental creativity and the search for luckier names will always make the thousands already in circulation seem too few. In a country jostling with Jóns and Guðrúns and Helgas, a Bambi, a Marzibil, a Sónata, is an invitation to admire and remember. But occasionally parental creativity tries too hard. Then Jóhannes must send the submission back, telling the petitioner to pick another name and to be more careful about the rules that he and his colleagues are bound to enforce. It is with such a message that the committee replies, in May 2016, to the couple who wrote in with *Cleopatra*. The name is turned down on the grounds that the letter *C* has no place in the Icelandic alphabet.

If, politically, Iceland has long been one of the world's most liberal nations—the first European state to give women the vote, an early adopter of marriage between same-sex partners, the sole to date whose government has been led by a lesbian—in matters of language it is highly conservative. Personal names—many of which date back to the sagas and comprise nouns and verbs and adjectives that speak of the long bleak winters communally, ancestrally, endured (*Eldjárn*, "fire iron"; *Glóbjört*, "glow bright")—are thought of as an extension of the language, part of the national patrimony. So Icelanders preserve their names as the English preserve their castles: Icelandic names, like England's historic buildings, are listed; the committee, like a heritage commission, is appointed every four years to supervise, adjudicate, oversee.

The present committee was appointed in 2014. Jóhannes, then forty-one, was young. But his credentials are impeccable. He has a doctorate in Icelandic grammar. He has authored many learned papers (in one, he categorized fifteen different sorts of hyphens: the hyphens that link compound nouns or digits written in words, that denote hesitation, that show elided pronunciation, and so on). And, perhaps most importantly, he has the best of all names. Jóhannes Bjarni Sigtryggsson. A name in keeping with his family tree. His grandfather—and not any old grandfather, a celebrated poet of children's verse—had been a Jóhannes Bjarni; like many firstborn Icelanders, Jóhannes was named after his grandfather (who, to judge by the black-and-white photographs, he somewhat resembles—a resemblance the grandson, with his mousy hair worn short and his round glasses, cultivates). The poet's daughter Þóra married a Sigtryggur, Jóhannes's father. Jóhannes Bjarni Sigtryggsson: grandson of Jóhannes Bjarni, son of Sigtryggur.

Jóhannes is married and has three sons. When they became parents, Jóhannes and his wife stuck to tradition rigorously. They named their eldest son Guðmundur after the boy's maternal grandfather; their second they named Sigtryggur in memory of Jóhannes's father. Out of grandfathers to name their third son after, Jóhannes and his wife chose to call him Eysteinn in honor of Eysteinn Ásgrímsson, a fourteenth-century monk and poet known for the purity of his Icelandic.

Icelandic "pure"? To the tourist for whom the country is all fairy-tale elves and unpronounceable volcanoes, the idea will be surprising. To a sympathetic outsider like myself, friendly with Icelanders from various walks of life, familiar with their language and landscape, it is more than surprising: it is absurd. Many in Iceland are far too playful with their words to handle them reverentially. Like the easygoing

Australians—those inhabitants of a hotter, vaster island—who, more than Britons or Americans, are fond of telescoping their commonest nouns (*relly* for *relative*, *ute* for *utility vehicle*, *ambo* for *ambulance*), Icelandic mouths are quick to dock lengthy words: *ammó* for *afmæli* ("birthday"), *fyrró* for *fyrramálið* ("tomorrow morning"). Readers of the popular broadsheet *Morgunblaðið* ask their newsagent for the "Mogga." The same goes for names. In Iceland everyone is on first-name terms. A Guðrún—the most popular girl's name in Iceland—is Guðrún even to five-minute acquaintances, even in the telephone directory (where *Jóhannes Bjarni Sigtryggsson, Icelandic specialist,* follows *Jóhannes Bjarni Eðvarðsson, mason,* and *Jóhannes Bjarni Jóhannesson, engineer*). But to her close friends and family, *Guðrún* ("Godly Mystery") is too formal: with a brother she answers instead to *Gurra*; to a childhood pal she will always be *Gunna; Rúna* is how an aunt on her father's side addresses her; another aunt, on the mother's side, calls her *Dunna.* And if this Gunna or Dunna comes from a village in the north, or from the Vestmannaeyjar, an archipelago off the south coast, she might be known as *Gunna lilla* ("little Gunna") if she is a short woman. Or if she is very thin, as *Dunna stoppnál* ("Darning needle Dunna"). If, working in a kitchen, she always has her sleeves rolled up, the villagers might call her *Gunna ermalausa* ("Sleeveless Gunna"). Our Jóhannes, the committee man, on the other hand, isn't anyone's *Jói*; and at the mere idea of *Hannes,* he frowns. *Jói orðabók* ("Dictionary Jói") or *Hannes nei nei* ("No, No Hannes") would make his thoughts crawl. To one and all, he is simply Jóhannes.

Jóhannes is a quiet man, a word puzzle fan, a vegetarian in a land of meat eaters. He wouldn't swat a fly. So he is unhappy when a decision by the committee leads to a parent's complaint in big and angry handwriting. He would like to tell the complainer, "I'm sorry. I didn't make the rules." The rules decide when he has to get out his red pencil. And Jóhannes is right. He didn't make the rules; they were already in place, more or less as they exist today, in his grandfather's time. The history of language purism in Iceland is long and complicated. Over the centuries, the form of this purism has changed. When Icelandic readers in the Middle Ages praised Eysteinn Ásgrímsson for the purity of his work, they meant to praise its Lutheran austerity, the spare lines shorn of affectation. Now when the academics praise someone's speech or writing as "pure," they mean it is an Icelandic unadulterated by foreign words, foreign sounds, foreign letters (like the C in *Cleopatra*). The shift requires a little explaining. To understand Icelandic purism in its modern form, with its strict rules and red pencils, it is necessary to look back to events in the early nineteenth century.

The young authors writing in Icelandic in the early 1800s wrote under the sway of Romanticism: they had a Romantic idea of their language's past. In their imaginations, Icelandic was a once beautiful woman who had taken to her sickbed, laid low by an infection of Low German, Latin, and Danish loanwords. Danish, in particular, the language of the island's colonizers, had weakened Icelandic. The authors, in their writings, sought to help their language convalesce. They mocked certain Danish sounds, the way the men and women in Copenhagen chewed their words. They lauded the old, weather-beaten farmers in the island's faraway villages who, they said, couldn't comprehend the slightest Danish. Soon, *Danish* became more than a word of nationalistic displeasure: to act Danish was to dandify your speech with Parisian salon talk, turn your back on the homeland, put on airs. To speak Icelandic in the capital, Reykjavík, while avoiding the temptations of fashionably French-sounding Danish, was to speak in the manner of an honest, upright man, sincerely and unself-consciously.

Iceland required the proud voice of a modern national poet, so the authors believed; the Germans had Goethe; the French had Molière; the English had Shakespeare. They promoted from their ranks a young naturalist by the name of Jónas Hallgrímsson. No one had written so beautifully about the island's fauna and flora before, nor so deftly sketched the ironies of everyday life for the little farmholder:

Hví svo þrúðgu þú
þokuhlassi,
súlda norn!
um sveitir ekur?
Þjér mun eg offra,
til árbóta
kú og konu
og kristindómi.

[Goddess of drizzle,
driving your big

cartloads of mist
across my fields!
Send me some sun
and I'll sacrifice
my cow — my wife —
my Christianity!]

Moreover, the naturalist showed a remarkable aptitude for inventing new words, words made out of existing words, without having to borrow sounds or notions from the obliging French, Greeks, or Danes. *Aðdráttarafl* ("magnetic force," literally "attraction power"), *fjaðurmagnaður* ("supple," literally "stretch-mighty"), *hitabelti* ("the Tropics," literally "heat-belt"), and *sjónarhorn* ("perspective," literally "sight corner") are only a few of the hundreds with which he endowed the language. Then, in 1845, he died at the age of thirty-eight, and his naively bucolic vision of his countrymen as wise farmer-citizens became forever fixed.

Icelandic is self-sufficient: this became the cry of the nationalists seeking independence from Denmark. Poetry reduced to politics. In 1918, independence came. But the aftereffects of Hallgrímsson's naive vision persisted. The national obsession with rooting out every trace of foreign influence in the language grew fierce. So fierce that from time to time government campaigns would lecture citizens on how to tell Icelandic, Danish, and other foreign words apart. Listen to *tónlist* (literally "tone-art"), newspaper readers were crisply informed, not *músík*. Take your shower in a *steypibað* (literally "pour-bath"), not in a *sturta*. *Smart*, the

Danish way of describing someone or something as "taste-ful," was repudiated in favor of *smekklegt*. And as technology expanded and the world shrank, the purists' efforts only intensified. The minting of brand-new words became a full-time occupation. Since the 1960s, the country's universities regularly put their eggheads together to rationalize the work. (The minutes of their meetings, like those of the Persons' Names Committee, are currently written by Jóhannes.) The work also includes keeping tabs on the media, lest a for-eign word — these days, usually English — supersede any Icelandic coinages. Upbraiding fingers will be wagged at the television or radio presenter who forgets to say *jafning-jaþrýstingur* instead of the current *peer-pressure*.

It is the paradox of the Romanticists' struggle that, though it was supposed to free the Icelander of all anxiety to perform, as well as erase any standards of speech beyond those words and sounds that come naturally to mind and tongue, the result has been quite the opposite. The poet and his pastoral vision, creating the ideal speaker, also created a new linguistic standard and divided the nation's consciousness. When those who live far from the countryside in the capital, as two-thirds now do, catch themselves saying something from an Ameri-can film, or a British pop song, they cringe. Some undergo a linguistic crisis and yearn for the best, the purest Icelandic, that Icelandic of Icelandics still spoken out in the sticks, to communicate authentically. It is of this yearning, the narra-tor's, that the popular, prizewinning novel *Góðir Íslendingar* (*Fellow Countrymen*), published in 1998, speaks: a forlorn young Reykjavík-dweller discovers a certain dignity — of speech, and thus of character—only among the isolated country folk (the translation is mine):

> Up to this day the best Icelandic in the land was said to be spoken in Hali [a tiny farming community in the south-east of the country]. I was filled with admiration when I stepped inside this temple of Icelandic.... the woman went over to the stove, stirred a large pot and made coffee.... when I mentioned having heard that here was spoken the most beautiful Icelandic in the country, the woman called over from the kitchen, "I don't know about that. Here we speak the East-Skaftafell dialect.... some men once came here and said that the folk over in Hestgirði spoke the purest."... I have become so self-conscious about my own speech that I turn every sentence over three times in my mind before I dare let it out.

"The best Icelandic in the land"—but the narrator's judgment isn't aesthetic, only notional. Not so much as a sentence of this "purest" dialect does he hear, and it doesn't matter. It is in this Icelandic-as-idea that the narrator, his author, and many readers feel great pride; in their own everyday Icelandic, many feel unsure. Somehow, the two Icelandics coexist.

It is in a present reflecting this history that the decisions of Jóhannes and his colleagues on the Persons' Names Committee make news. Headlines like *"Manuel* and *Tobbi* get the green light, but not *Dyljá"* and *"Yngveldur* is allowed, but *Swanhildi* is banned"* are common. The article under the former, published in May 2016, notes that the committee has adjusted the final names of four children of immigrant parents: "the son of Petar is now Pétursson, the daughter of Joao becomes Jónsdóttir, the son of Szymonar, Símonarson, and Ryszard's daughter becomes Ríkharðsdóttir." In the previous month, articles relayed the committee's curious decision to authorize the boy's name *Ugluspegill* (literally "Owl Mirror") — an adaptation of a name for a prankster in medieval German folklore. "Whilst indications exist that the name has negative connotations in Icelandic," the committee conceded in its report, "these are little known among the general public and aren't for that matter particularly negative or derogatory." The committee concluded, "A remote or uncertain risk that the name will cause its bearer embarrassment in the future is not sufficient reason to ban it. We therefore give the name *Ugluspegill* the benefit of the doubt."

Reports like this have fostered anger toward the committee, which has been growing in some quarters of the country. Every now and then Jóhannes hears of a public figure who wants to see the committee closed down and Icelanders allowed to name their offspring however they like, but he only shakes his head doubtfully. He recalls what his colleague Ágústa says when she hears this kind of talk: wind us down and you'll end up with families that give their children only digits for names, and others that will want to go by an appellation seventeen names long. Above all else, Jóhannes and his colleagues worry for Icelandic grammar. In Icelandic, nouns have gender. Boys' names behave like masculine nouns, girls' names like feminine nouns. But how to determine the correct declensions of names like Tzvi, Qillaq, Çağrı? What if immigrant parents bestow on their son a name which, to Icelandic eyes, has the forms of a girl's? Jóhannes puts on a brave face, but he worries.

He has reason to worry. In 2012, an adolescent's parents took an old decision by the committee to court in an attempt to overturn it. Jóhannes's predecessors told the court they had simply followed the rules. They explained how the confusion in the case had all begun. One day, fifteen years ago, when they were in their little room at the registry building going through their post, a priest's baptismal paperwork caught their eyes. They assumed that the priest had messed up the forms. They telephoned the parsonage. No, the priest responded, he had not. He had written *Blær* in the space for the infant's name, and he had meant to write *Blær*, because it was thus that the baby girl had been christened. The committee members stopped him there. They were grammar-bound, they said, to invalidate the name: *Blær*, though the noun sounds sweetly, and though it means "gentle breeze," is masculine. A masculine noun for a baby girl! What had he been thinking? The priest apologized: the name was so rare—apparently there are only five men named Blær in all of Iceland—that he hadn't given the matter proper thought. He tried to broker a compromise; the priest and the parents talked. But when he suggested fine-tuning the newborn's name to *Blædís,* a perfectly good girl's name, the couple would not hear of it.

The mother, Björk Eiðsdóttir, told the court her side of the story. She said she had found the name Blær in the much-loved 1957 novel *Brekkukotsannáll* (*The Fish Can Sing*), by Halldór Laxness. (Mischievous, prickly, gifted Laxness is the country's only Nobel Prize in Literature laureate. As a young man, he changed his own name from Halldór Guðjónsson. As an author, he had no time for the language purists. The spelling in his novels had always been his own: he wrote *leingi* instead of *lengi* ["a long time"] and *sosum* instead of *svo sem* ["about, roughly"], adhering closer to how the words are pronounced. And his novels frequently mocked the purists' naive Romanticism, tempering their pristine flower-colored valleys with tales of rural destitution and sheep diarrhea.) Laxness, in typical Laxness fashion, had made the Blær of his novel a female character; and Björk Eiðsdóttir decided that if she ever had a daughter she would call her Blær. In 1997 her daughter was born and baptized. When told by the priest that the committee was unhappy with her choice of name and had rejected it, she wrote pleading letters to the prime minister and the archbishop in vain. Five years later, when the family traveled to the United States, the girl's passport gave her legal identity as Stúlka ("Girl"). It was like a game. Whenever she stood before a uniform she was Stúlka, but with her parents, teachers, and classmates she was always Blær. Her mother added, pointedly, that her daughter had often been complimented on her name. Now the girl was fifteen. Before very long she would marry and pass the name down to her own children. It was why mother and daughter had finally decided to sue.

When the solicitor general summed up on behalf of the committee, he allowed that *Blær* sounds less masculine than many other words. Even so, he said, it would represent a "big step" for the court to determine that nothing prevented *Blær* from belonging to a child of either sex.

The lawyer representing the girl and her mother replied with a flourish. He said that the step the court was being asked to take was really rather small, since, as it turned out, there existed precedent in Iceland for calling a girl Blær: a Blær Guðmundsdóttir, born in 1973 (only a few months after Jóhannes), already appeared in the national registry. This Blær's mother had persuaded the committee there was a set of possible feminine declensions of the noun: if a woman called Blær gave you a gift, it would be from *Blævi* (whereas from a man called Blær it would be from *Blæ*); if you hadn't seen the same woman for some time you could say that you missed *Blævar* (whereas if your absent friend was a man you would be missing, *Blæs*). Icelandic grammar, the lawyer concluded, was malleable. Societies change; their grammars change.

The court agreed. In January 2013 the judge, over the committee's misgivings, awarded the girl the right to go henceforth by the name of Blær.

Societies change. A hundred years ago children born out of wedlock were a rarity in Iceland. Today the opposite is increasingly true. No stigma attaches to the Icelandic mother who raises a child by herself. For this reason, among others, more and more sons incorporate the mother's name into their surname.

Grammars change. The obsolescence of the committee is only a question of time. Twenty years from now, or twenty-five, or thirty, a young man will walk among his country's fjords, gullies, and glaciers. He will be called Antónius Cleopötruson.

Nine

DEAD MAN TALKING

The man at the Manx language museum was enthusiastic, more than pleased to help; and within days of my electronic inquiry there arrived in the mail a copy of *Skeealyn Vannin* (*Isle of Man Stories*). The museum's pride these stories are, each told, in the words of the island's last native speakers, into recording machines seventy years ago and ever since preserved on acetate, then cassette, now digitally remastered, transcribed, and translated into English. Thick, big, and dense—hardly light reading material—the resulting collection, with its accompanying CDs, testifies to the compilers' tremendous dedication. The thought of this labor, that of a critically endangered language's tiny band of revivalists, was astonishing. How many unearning hours they had lavished on the collection's every voice, every page, every paragraph! Thanks to them, through death and decades of general indifference the stories had survived. They had come down to me, an Englishman in Paris, in a crumpled orange envelope postmarked at Douglas, the island's capital, intact. I handled the book reverentially. It promised revival, a reprieve from extinction; but can such a promise be kept? About it hung an unmistakable air of elegy. On the cover, black-and-white photographs of flat-capped, watery-eyed elders stared out at me.

Mann, or the Isle of Man, is a small island—220 square miles, no bigger than Guam—in the middle of the Irish Sea. Ireland lies west; head due north and you'll make land in Scotland. To the south, at a farther distance than these other neighbors, is the other nation where a Celtic language is still widely spoken, Wales. The Celts settled Mann around the sixth century CE. The island was wind, rock, and ragwort; it was also, tradition tells us, fairies. The *mooinjer veggey* (literally, "little people"), the isle's original possessors, had protected its shores from Rome by shrouds of a magical mist.

For centuries, history—Catholic saints, Norse berserkers, English nobles—came and went. History long ignored the Manxman's language. The island's stones were good only for runes, parchment only for Latin. Manx shouts and sweet nothings, calls and compliments, jokes and jeers, rose and vanished into the air like fairy mist. It wasn't until after the Reformation that local clergy began committing Manx prayers to paper, began easing their parishioners' sounds into a readable and reproducible script. In a bilingual 1707 tract entitled *The Principles and Duties of Christianity/Coyrle Sodjeh*, the language attained at last the dignity of print. Years later, a Manx translation of the Gospels followed. But the church didn't publish Manx for the sake of elevating the language; the island's religious leader, the Englishman Thomas Wilson, thought it beneath his bishop's dignity to speak it with any fluency. The real reason Manx got published was that so few of the islanders could read and comprehend English. An English vicar at the pulpit mouthing away like a fish plucked out of water, intelligible only by virtue of his familiar, dainty, slender-fingered gestures, the regularity of his droning, the occasional "Jesus" and "amen": this, in certain parishes, was the Sunday sermon. As late as 1842, in a letter to the isle's lieutenant governor, a group of clergy was compelled to write, "In all the parishes of the island there are many persons who comprehend no other language than Manx.... An acquaintance with this language is a qualification indispensably requisite in those who minister."

But by then the islanders' language had already gone into decline and was retreating fast for the hills of villages. It was described as "decaying" by its first lexicographer, Archibald Cregeen, in the introduction to his Manx-English dictionary:

> I am well aware that the utility of the following work will be variously appreciated by my brother Manksmen. Some will be disposed to deride the endeavor to restore vigor to a decaying language. Those who reckon the extirpation of the Manks a necessary step toward the general extension of the English, which they deem essential to the interest of the Isle of Man, will condemn every effort which seems likely to retard its extinction.

The deriders were in the capital, the merchants and their customers: English speakers through and through, and eager importers of all things British. For generations, their small population held steady; their urban condescension toward the provincials remained limited. Then the nineteenth century brought with it the international craze for sea bathing. Suddenly, sand and salt breezes were commodities. Mann possessed both in abundance. The numbers of English speakers visiting the island swelled.

So that after history — its saints and berserkers and nobles — tourism (a new word) now came to Mann. The tourists outnumbered the natives two, then three, then five, then ten to one. They were families from Britain's northern mill towns for the most part. On holiday. Full of chat. Soon the island's towns grew noisy with them speaking English. Not the English of the islanders' vicars, mind you, all drone punctuated by the occasional *amen;* theirs was musical, easygoing, moneyed. The islanders in their woolen jumpers, on hearing the tourist talk, began to itch. They began to cross over to English whenever a vacationer walked into earshot. And so, little by little, the Manx people lost touch with their language.

Losing touch with the Manx language meant forfeiting its own peculiar treasure. Hundreds of years' worth of accumulated knowledge, each speaker's birthright, was jettisoned. The language had nurtured health. A great-grandmother, knowing the Manx for this plant or that flower, the traditional names transforming each into a potential remedy, might cure generations of her family of wheezy coughs, gammy legs, upset stomachs. It had promised boys adventure at sea and put food on the table. It had

incited complicity—in endearments and turns of phrase—
even between a farmer and his animals. "In my youthful
days it was in Manx we always spoke to our horses and our
cows. Even the dogs themselves, unless you spoke to them
in Manx, couldn't understand you," wrote J. T. Clarke in
1872. All this, with every speaker's death, fell a little further
out of everyday currency and into the realm of folklore.

At the last count, the 2011 census, barely one fiftieth of
the island, which comes to a little over 1,800 inhabitants,
claimed any knowledge of Manx. Of these, maybe several
score—the most ardent revivalists—could speak the language more or less fluently. The numbers are catastrophic; it
is a measure of the revivalists' ardor that they are yet able to
read in them a sort of triumph. And it is true, the numbers
are less catastrophic than they were a generation or two ago.
They represent an improvement from the 1940s, when
hardly one person in every hundred knew any Manx at all. It
was during those bleak years that the revivalists recorded
the stories of the island's last native speakers.

Yn Cheshaght Ghailckagh, the Manx Language Society,
the revivalists called themselves. They were bookish, bril-
liantined young men who spent their weekends foraging for
the last natives in the outlying farms and villages. Every
rumor was pursued, every suggested name taken seriously.
Doors of thatched cottages were knocked on; respondents
were addressed in Manx, and, often, quickly apologized to
in English. But there were also times—each a cause for
relief and joy—when, after tramping across marshy fields or
noticing some out-of-the-way turning in one of the isle's

many nooks and crannies, a white-haired native Manxman or -woman was stumbled upon. Then the young men would bring out their pencils and notebooks and prod the old speakers' memories with their questions: What could they remember about their schooldays? In what ways had the village changed in the past fifty or sixty years? Did they recall the Manx word for this bird or that vegetable? Any proverbs? Could they recite the Lord's Prayer? The young revivalists would visit the friendliest, or perhaps loneliest, speakers regularly. Some apprenticed themselves to the speakers' farms in return for several hours of conversational Manx per week. In this way the revivalists—future teachers at evening classes in the language—fine-tuned their accents, fleshed out their vocabularies, became more and more conversant.

Consternated too. Time was pressing; the speakers were frail and very old. Before long the revivalists would be out of native voices to listen to. So they set to recording them, committing the voices to a revolving disk, for the benefit of future learners. A recording van—a gracious loan from the Irish government—duly arrived on a cattle boat from Dublin on April 22, 1948. After hosing it clean of dung, the young men drove off on a tour that would take them up and down the island, from village to village, for the next two weeks.

Fear of failure must have been distracting. Bad roads awaited them; plentiful spring rain—drumming, voluble—threatened interruption after interruption; the 12-inch acetate disks (with space on each side for fifteen minutes of recording) were prone to blips. But the speakers' frailty was uppermost in the young men's anxieties. The speakers had gotten to an age at which their cottages possessed lives of their own. Water in a saucepan would occasionally boil by itself. Knitting needles would somehow find their way into a cutlery drawer. And in conversation the elders' attention frequently wandered. Dialogue was ever fraught. Words were left hanging in the air, suspended in mid-sentence. An answer proffered might return minutes afterward. Also, what would they make of the newfangled technology? They had never seen a turntable in their lives. Some of the cottages weren't even equipped with electricity. (In those cases, the men had to shepherd the occupants in their van to one that was.) What if they proved shy of microphones?

Shy as Mrs. Kinvig. Pushing eighty. A smart, small-featured crofter who read the Manx Bible every day. She had raised ten predominantly English speakers in the tiny southern hamlet of Ronague. The surrounding countryside Mrs. Kinvig knew like the back of her hand. She knew the spot near the hamlet where spilled water appeared to roll uphill. She knew the best place to catch sight and smell of the steam train bound for the capital. She knew the way to Castletown, an hour's journey on foot across sodden fields to the coast (a journey she had undertaken every morning as a young dressmaker). Her Manx, of the nineteenth century, she had acquired quite by chance; it was what her parents spoke whenever they wished to discuss something unintended for their daughter's ears. In her old age, between snipping turnips and tossing chicken feed, Mrs. Kinvig kept up her Manx with Mr. Kinvig, ten years her senior, and with the young revivalists who dropped in from time to time. But now when the men came in the van and asked her to repeat, from her store of anecdotes, their favorites, Mrs. Kinvig grew tight-lipped. The microphone intimidated. No amount of encouragement from the men or her husband would coax the stories out of her. Finally, though, she relented — whether from fatigue or sheer embarrassment — and called up from memory several hymns:

Dy hirveish Jee dy jeean, [A charge to keep I have]
Shoh'n raaue va currit dou, [A God to glorify]
Dy yannoo ellan veen, [A never-dying soul to save]
Dy chiartagh ee son niau. [And fit it for the sky]

The recorders had better luck with the oldest Manxman, John Kneen of Ballaugh in the north, who was closing in on his hundredth birthday (and who, as it happened, had another ten years in him). *Yn Gaaue*, the smith, the villagers called him. Gnarled fingers resting on his walking stick, Kneen reminisced aloud about his years shoeing horses *"son daa skillin 's kiare pingyn son y kiare crouyn"* ("for two shillings and four pence for the four shoes"), when there were thirty smithies in the north and *"cha row treiney, ny boult, ny red erbee cheet voish Sostyn"* ("there wasn't a nail, nor bolt, nor anything coming from England"). To provide the smith with a conversation mate, the recorders fetched another Manx native, Harry Boyde, a former laborer; though lifelong neighbors — their cottages only five miles apart — the two men had never spoken before. Introductions must have gone well, for they spoke together in Manx for hours to the delight of the recorders who had them sit equidistant from the Mrs. Kinvig–scaring microphone. With the young men, Kneen had often been loquacious; with Boyde now he turned suddenly attentive: peering out of his one good eye, a veiny hand cupping his working ear, he let his interlocutor do much of the talking, content to nudge one or another of Boyde's recollections along every now and then with a *"Dy jarroo, ghooinney?"* ("Really, man?") or a *"Nagh vel eh?"* ("Is it not?"). The men talked manure and rum and market life. They described an island on which booted feet had been splayed by riding horses, the riders little more than their titles: *yn saggyrt* ("the parson"), *yn cleragh* ("the clerk"). They told their stories without inhibition, with the great unself-consciousness of the ancient. They thought back over their long lives to times when emotions ran highest. Kneen, loquacity returning to him, left Boyde to listen in amazement as he nonchalantly recalled having once seen a crowd of fairies, the little people, leap and frolic in the meadow at sundown: *"Va'n fer mooar gollrish mwaagh"* ("the big one was like a hare"). At the sound of the blacksmith, the fairies started and fled.

From Ballaugh the young men continued on the last leg of their tour of the island. They drove to the northernmost tip to record a brother and sister, John Tom Kaighin and Annie Kneale. Of Kaighin one of the recorders wrote in his notebook: "Blind, aged 85, very lively and with an enormous voice." Something of this liveliness is communicated in his story about the parson and the pig. One evening, at dinnertime, a parson came to the home of an old woman parishioner. He saw a pig eating out of a pot on the kitchen floor. The old woman invited the parson to sit, but the parson refused to sit unless she first *"cur y muc shen magh"* ("put that pig out"). The woman repeated her invitation, feigning calm and deafness; the parson refused to sit; the pig tucked into his pot. On and on this went, until at last, the parson snapped the old woman's patience: *"Cha jean mee cur y muc magh"* ("I won't put the pig out"), she blurted, since the pig at least brought money into the household, whereas the parson took it out.

Annie Kneale had a harder time than her brother in recollecting her Manx. Forgetfulness occasionally got the better of her. Her speaking was rusty. Sometimes she would lapse into English; a sentence begun in Manx might conclude in English. But she wasn't one to despair. And the young men were encouraging. Adroitly, they rephrased a question or overlooked a fumble; proffered words supplemented her sketchy responses. Vivid fragments of a former existence, with the men's help, gradually resurfaced. Girlhood memories: village folk, when the wind dropped, saying *"T'eh geaishtagh"* ("It's listening"); her mother, when porridge on the stove started to bubble, saying *"T'eh sonsheraght"* ("It's whispering"), then *"T'eh sonsheraght, gow jeh eh. T'eh jeant nish"* ("Take it off [the heat], it's done now"). Glimpses of a lost way of life, a vanished world in which even the wind and the porridge spoke Manx.

The year after the recording Annie Kneale died. She was survived by eight known native speakers.

To listen to the recordings at a lifetime's remove, in the warm and dry of a Parisian apartment, having fed the bright CDs into a modern player, was to complicate sentimentality. And yet the old men's and women's voices, as they filled my living room, moved me. The voices held frailty, but also a certain sly humor. In spite of the words lost in beards or expelled as whistles through missing teeth, they were strangely attractive. More than once, listening intently, I caught myself mouthing along.

I kept an eye on the transcripts as I listened. The words made me think of Welsh: the verb-first sentences, concatenations of consonants that intimidated the tongue, the sophisticated ballet of sounds hard and soft. The Welsh of my weeklong vacations. Road signs in Wales — *ysgol* ("school"), *canol y dref* ("town center"), *gyrrwch yn ddiogel* ("drive safely") — wouldn't have looked out of place on the island, I thought. I could almost envision the Eisteddfod, a large Welsh music and poetry festival, taking place on Mann.

When Brian Stowell was sixteen, he read in a local newspaper about the imminent demise of Manx. He got in touch with the article's author, a young revivalist by the name of Douglas Fargher, and joined the cause. Ten years later, in 1964, the two would drive south along gorse-lined roads into Glen Chass ("Sedge Valley") to tape the last native Manx-man standing (and speaking).

"I got my Manx from the same men who had met and recorded the native speakers in 1948," Brian tells me by telephone. The continuity is important to him; it confers authority. It is with an air of authority, briskly, that he speaks. "Conversed every weekend with Doug. A live wire, he was. Had a fruit import business in the capital. Every weekend, long conversations with him and his workmates: six hours of spoken Manx on a Saturday; four to six hours on a Sunday. By the following Easter I was speaking the language fluently."

Glen Chass was home to Edward "Ned" Maddrell, a retired fisherman who had been the youngest of the 1948 speakers. In 1964 he was in his eighty-seventh year. Black-and-white photographs, and the odd color Polaroid, of Ned Maddrell—all findable on the Internet—show a large man, broad-shouldered. His frame suggests a lifetime of manual labor, but he also seems to have been something of a snappy dresser—always in a shirt and tie—and approachable. A ruddy face handsome with composure. To his upbringing by a great-aunt, and the relative reclusion of a subsequent life at sea, Maddrell owed his Manx speaking. He could remember his childhood, when everyone in the village spoke Manx to each other. Not to speak it was to be an oddity, like a person deaf and mute. He could remember old Mrs. Keggin, who lived in a thatched cottage at the foot of the road leading to Cronk ny Arrey Laa, and who had no English. (According to Professor Sir John Rhys of Celtic at Oxford, she was probably the last Manx monoglot.) Through Ned—whose schooling was in English—Mrs. Keggin would barter her eggs for rolls every week with the traveling bread man.

Maddrell didn't let his being the language's safekeeper go to his head (though the attentions of the young revivalists, linguists, and the occasional journalist — some from afar — must have sweetened his final years). Brian recalls the courtesy with which he and his colleague were greeted and welcomed into the largish room that served as Maddrell's reception area. The two men came with cassette tapes — still a novelty in the 1960s — and eyed the turning spools as they and Maddrell, in facing armchairs, conversed. Perhaps to an outsider it might have seemed that they had come to take down Manx's dying words. But their conversation in the language, regularly punctured by light banter and gentle laughter, asserted optimism: Manx, in the shape of Brian and the other revivalists, would go on being heard and spoken long into the future; the succession was assured.

In spite of his great age and native credentials, Maddrell, with the young men, was modesty itself. He wouldn't speak in the manner of a master addressing his disciples. On the contrary, he deferred continuously to their education. "If I make a mistake, don't hesitate in correcting me," Maddrell told them in English at one point. "You're scholars, and I'm not." The deference posed its own risks.

"We wanted to double-check the correct pronunciation of *eayn*, meaning 'lamb,'" Brian tells me. "We asked Ned to say the Manx for *lamb* aloud. Ned said '*eayn*.' My colleague, Doug, repeated what Ned had just said, but it came out a bit differently. Ned said, 'That's it,' and then imitated Doug's pronunciation. But we were aware of this sort of hazard."

There were surprises. To the revivalists, who had thirty

years of Manx learning between them, some of the old man's words and expressions were new. Maddrell was talking about his days and nights aboard rocking boats, amid nets and lazy crabs and low skies, when for "star" he said *roltag*. But the dictionary's version was *rollage*—appearing right after its definition of *rollag*: "the hollow an oar works in on the gunwale of a boat." Had the old man made a slip of the tongue? Brian and his colleague knew otherwise. They knew that Maddrell's boat had brought him into regular contact with Irish sailors. For "star" the sailors would have used their Gaelic word, *réalta*. Maddrell's Manx had simply adjusted to its environment, to the Irish sailors' comprehension; *roltag* was among the adjustments that had stuck. Equally unfamiliar was the expression of Maddrell's *"Va ny taareeyn er"* ("The terrors were upon him")—an inheritance, it turned out, from Old Irish.

For many years after Maddrell's death in 1974, Brian assumed custody of Manx. He worked by day as a physics lecturer "across the water" in Merseyside, and then in the evening devised distance courses in the language and wrote promotional articles and sang traditional ballads for a vinyl LP. To remedy the lack of Manx literature—"The Bible is no use, too difficult"—he translated popular children's tales. In 1990 his *Contoyryssyn Ealish ayns Cheer ny Yindyssyn* (*Alice's Adventures in Wonderland*) appeared. By that time attitudes toward the language had long softened to bemusement; it became possible for the island's schoolchildren to be taught a smattering of Manx.

Brian: "Many pupils were learning French or Spanish

already. To these, teachers began adding thirty minutes of Manx per week. A few words one lesson, the odd phrase the next. Nothing strenuous. The parents didn't object."

So, having learned to say *Je m'appelle Jean* or *Me llamo Juan,* and to count *un, deux, trois, quatre, cinq,* or *uno, dos, tres, cuatro, cinco,* the pupils were taught to say *Ta'n ennym orrym John* and to count *nane, jees, tree, kiare, queig.* But not much else. Manx materials—books, exercises, trained teachers— were still in very short supply. The lessons were like the small change of the foreign language departments' resources.

The revivalists did not mind. The thought of children speaking any Manx at all delighted them. Brian explains:

> Remember, not long before, most islanders had given up on the language. Manx had a reputation problem. It was associated with poor people and backwardness. Then it was associated with loners and eccentricity. We were embarrassed to speak it in front of others. I have a little story about that. I rang a pal on the island one day from my home in Liverpool. I spoke as usual in Manx, but he would only answer in English. If I said something like "kys t'ou?" he'd reply, a little stiffly, "Fine, thanks, how are you?" It was only afterward that I realized that my friend had been at work when I called. He had an office job. He didn't want his col- leagues to hear him using Manx.

Brian gives me another story from around the same period: pub-goers who conversed over their beers in Manx sometimes found themselves on the receiving end of another drinker's anger, he said. Insults had been known to ignite into brawls.

Such incidents are now behind the revivalists, Brian says. He has seen for himself how much things have changed in the twenty-five years since he left England and physics and retired to Mann. People from all over the island show growing interest in the language; the number of learners rises census by census. The obstacles to revival no longer seem insuperable. Only, the workload has become too much for Brian. Some years ago, he handed the work over to Adrian Cain—an energetic forty-something. Among the revivalists, Brian and Adrian are household names.

Shortly after talking to Brian, I telephone Adrian to learn more about him and contemporary Manx. "I'm originally from the south of the island, near Cregneash, Ned Maddrell's natal village. I had aunts who told of the scraps of Manx they heard around them growing up." Much like Brian, he fell in with the revivalists as a teenager, and their zeal rubbed off on him; learning the language took up much of his early adulthood; years later, he wrote in it to Manx friends from the desk of his economics classroom in east London. In London, for a time, he got caught up in city politics—"left-wing type stuff"—but quite soon he tired of the marches and slogans. His thoughts turned to home. "I thought, defending a language is political. Not the signing of petitions and the like. The speaking and the teaching. Showing that Manx still matters. That's enough politics for me." His return coincided with the growing media market for "minority languages"; Manx, the fight to revive it, was suddenly newsworthy. Eager to talk up the cause, he gave interviews to reporter after reporter. "Cats with no tails, motorbike races, offshore accounting—it was all that most people had heard about the island. The language offered another side."

I ask him whether he finds the media tiring—that is, frustrating and disappointing. I can imagine that he is asked the same questions over and over.

"In a word, yes. Well, quite often. With some of the journalists' questions, you think, 'Oh my god, where do you start?'"

Adrian's Manx fluency once earned him a spot on a British teatime television program. He shared the sofa with a husky comedian of Caribbean descent. To the viewer, the contrast could hardly have been more startling. Just as noticeable was the language difference: the comedian's English boomed; Adrian's Manx sounded out of place. An hour before the program, in the green room, he had agreed when the producer instructed him to perform a crash course in the language. But now, on air, it happened that the host and the comedian had almost no time—literally—for the course. For all Adrian tried to talk concretely, to enthuse, in the few minutes allotted to him, the men's involvement remained half-hearted, their responses glib.

The experience, alas, is not uncommon. Adrian, all earnestness, accepts the invitation of a Belgian documentary maker, or a German press columnist, or a British radio host. He prepares for his bit part with care. He thinks up a num-

ber of good lines and simple examples. He irons his interview best. He arrives at the café or studio on the dot. He
hopes only that the interviewer will do the language justice.
But more often than not, the interviewer is late, heedless of
the scene-setting that would engage a wide audience, and
scantily prepped. Unsurprisingly, the result is a rushed,
cobbled-together cliché: the language of the islanders is as
hard to learn as it is quaintly exotic; its decline is sad; against
all the odds it resists doughtily. It is enough to depress any
revivalist. Worse, within a community as tiny as the islanders', jealousies talk. "Some say of me, 'There's Adrian again
in the media bigging himself up.'"

But Adrian prefers to remain upbeat. He is a professional
optimist. All publicity, to his mind, is good publicity. Publicity attracts learners from overseas, a new type of visitor —
the "linguistic tourist" (a boon to the island's economy,
which has suffered from the modern rise of cheap package
holidays to Spain). A bilingual *No Smoking* sign — *Jaaghey
Meelowit* — on a red-bricked street corner is to these tourists what a sea view was to Victorian vacationers.

"They are mostly young and come from all over Europe.
The idea of Manx as a community anyone can choose to
belong to is probably the principal draw. Our classes are very
relaxed. In a way we're all learners. There's no one right
accent to acquire: the German learners speak Manx with a
German accent, the Swedes with a Swedish accent, the
Czechs with a Czech accent. And that's fine."

Backpacks, long blond hair, middle-class giggles: Adrian's conversation groups are a world away from the farmers

and fishermen in their cottages. The new speakers' disparateness can occasionally strain a listener's comprehension. Adrian insists his learners have the freedom of the language.

"Some people have gotten quite into the old recordings of the native speakers and too involved in the small print of pronunciation. But ought we really to stick to 1940s fishing village pronunciations into the twenty-first century? Take *maynrey*, which means 'happy.'"

He says it "man-ra."

"Well, there are those who listen to the old recordings and hear 'mehn-ra.' They think everyone should say 'mehn-ra.' They say I'm saying and teaching it wrong. But the recordings are a tool, they're not gospel. 'Man-ra' is my dialect of Manx. I say 'man-ra,' you say 'mehn-ra.' It's all good. I suppose I'm a bigger-picture person: as long as you make out what I'm saying, and I what you're saying, our Manx is correct."

When he says this, I remember an argument among the revivalists over "correctness" that Brian mentioned. Fifty years ago, many new words needed coining to match modern island life: the elders of the recordings had never ridden in a car or airplane, owned a computer, or gone to university. Several revivalists responded by putting forward their own ideas for this or that word. Adrian anticipates my question.

"It's like *parallelogram*. Is that a Manx word? I don't know what else to call it. I would just say 'parallelogram.' Same for *jungle*. I say 'jungle.' The geekier, into-authenticity types say '*doofyr*.' They take it from Irish. Both words ought to be acceptable."

Grammar, too, can vary from speaker to speaker. Sentences are often simplified. Take a sentence like "I saw her yesterday." A fluent Manx speaker would say it *Honnick mee ee jea.* (*Honnick* is the irregular past tense form of *fakin* ["to see"]). Most learners, however, prefer to drop the irregular form and say instead *Ren mee fakin ee jea* ("I did see her yesterday"). Likewise for *Hie mee* ("I went"), which they replace with *Ren mee goll* ("I did go"). And, being "came" (*haink*) droppers, they say instead *Ren mee çheet* ("I did come").

"If Ned Maddrell or any of the other native speakers could be resuscitated and returned to the island today, they'd be astonished by the sight of these learners. The accents, some of the sentences, would probably strike them as rather odd. But they'd recognize the language as theirs. They'd understand and be understood when they spoke."

Regularly, Adrian does the next best thing to resuscitating the dead: starting with Brian, he confers with the few elders, not native speakers but nonetheless fluent, who still remember them. Like the recorders before him, he preserves every anecdote he hears. Half a century ago, Brian tape-recorded his conversation with Ned Maddrell; these days, Adrian videotapes his conversations with Brian and uploads them to the Internet — complete with subtitles — for all to watch.

I watch Brian and the other men in Adrian's videos, watch their brows pucker with reminiscence as they talk. There is Davy Quillin of Port Erin, gray-haired, blue-jeaned, his posture sagging into his burgundy sofa, talking about going to sea at sixteen with his Manx lesson books. He gestures toward his books under a coffee table, just out of eyeshot. He speaks his Manx quickly, fluently, the way he once heard it spoken as a child. He remembers well the day when, on a walk with his father, he spotted two old men three-legged with walking sticks. When he and his father got closer, he heard his father whisper "Listen." The old men, deep in conversation, were *"loayrt cho aashagh ass yn Ghaelg . . . v'eh yindyssagh clashtyn ad"* ("speaking so easily in Manx . . . it was wonderful to hear them"). One of the men was Ned Maddrell. He doesn't know who the other man was. *"Garroo,"* Maddrell and the other man kept repeating, as the weather beat about them: "Rough."

In another of Adrian's videos, Derek Philips, bald and bespectacled, white-mustached, with the fleshy look of a retired butcher, reclines in his cream sofa and demonstrates his grasp of Manx. His Manx, he explains, dates back to the revivalists' evening classes he sat in half a century ago. One of the revivalists, a Port Erin bank manager, befriended him; thereafter, they would meet regularly in each other's homes and converse in nothing but the language. Philips's nearness to fluency made him gregarious. He was always on the lookout for other speakers. Once, from behind the shop counter, he ventured to ask an elderly customer whether he knew any Manx. He was hoping to at least cadge a new word or two. But the customer replied with indignation, "Manx? Manx? That's nonsense, man. Manx is worthless!" He thinks the poor man must have had his Manx beaten out of him as a boy.

The videos — tens of minutes, all told, and mostly recorded in the intimacy of the elders' homes — offer a fair sample of modern Manx. For all their fluency, the men's lack of immersion in a community of speakers sometimes shows. Talking about gardening, Philips's lips pause before continuing with *poanraghyn* ("runner beans"). A moment later, he asks Adrian *"Cre t'an fockle son cauliflower?"* ("What's the word for cauliflower?"). *Laueanyn* — the Manx equivalent of "gloves" — is something he will misremember. He is at his best, his smoothest, when delivering any of his striking anecdotes; by dint of repetition over the years he tells them at an impressive rate.

One anecdote stands out in particular. In the pub one evening, a darts player came over and asked him for a game. In a minute or two, said Philips. I'm just talking to the wife. The player nodded and returned to his darts; he was about to fling one when he collapsed before the board. Philips's wife was a nurse. She ran over and *"prowal dy yannoo yn stoo er y cleeu echey"* ("tried to do the stuff on his chest"). In vain. The player was dead. Hastily the pub was emptied of its drinkers; an ambulance was called. And as the Philipses waited for the sirens, thirty minutes or so after the darts player's collapse, his body briefly made as if to sit up. *"As dooyrt my ven dooys, va shen yn aer scapail woish"* ("And my wife said, that was the air escaping from him").

At the ring of the bell, the blue uniformed pupils of the Bunscoill Ghaelgagh primary school race each other out of their classrooms into the playground. Some kick a ball; some skip rope; some stand about and chat. The teachers, all ears, walk among them, always on their guard. If they catch any chatterers whispering in English, they stop and issue a gentle rebuke.

The Bunscoill, which was founded in 2001 by a handful of parents, is situated in the island's central valley and is the first Manx-language school. In fifteen years, its intake (ages ranging from five to eleven) has expanded from scanty to seventy. A fair number of the current pupils' parents aren't revivalists; they hope that primary education in a second language will make their offspring future wizzes at Spanish, German, or French. The revivalists, for their part, hope the school demonstrates that Manx has a future: if seventy children is not exactly a big number, it is at least seventy more than are studying in the recently extinct languages Klallam (of North America), Pazeh (of Asia), or Nyawaygi (of Australia).

Among the newcomers to the school last year was Adrian's son, Orry. Orry has a head start on most of his schoolmates; Manx has been instilled in him by his father from birth. At six, he is still small; he makes a small child's mistakes. He can mix up *eayst* ("moon") and *eeast* ("fish"). "And one time we were on holiday in Norwich, and I said to my son '*Vel oo fakin yn shirragh shen ayns yn edd echey heose sy cheeill?*' ('Do you see that falcon in the nest up in the church?'), and he looked at me all confused and asked what the bird was doing in a hat. You see, *edd* can mean 'nest' but also 'hat.'" Such mistakes are a young native speaker's rite of passage to fluency. Orry grows surer-tongued by the day.

Orry and his schoolmates are the first children to speak

fluent Manx in over a hundred years. Visiting elders can hardly believe their ears when they sit in during lessons and hear the language in children's voices. Ditties and nursery rhymes unsung for generations have been given a second life; tales of modern life — of picnics, pop music, and computer games — fill sheets of paper before being read aloud.

The school employs four teachers and two class assistants. It isn't easy to find the staff. By some accounts, past class assistants have been far from word perfect. One of the newer teachers — a mother of pupils at the school — confided her pre-job interview nerves to a local reporter: she had had to brush up her grammar. For weeks prior to the interview, she had read nothing but Manx translations of children's books.

The headmistress gazes out of the windows at the passing traffic. Nearly everything beyond the school's weathered gray slate walls — tearoom sandwich boards, bus shelter graffiti, turned-on TVs, labels on milk bottles and cereal boxes and bags of sweets — is in English. English daily dwarfs the Manx that the children learn at school. English at the breakfast table, English outside the school gates, English during the bedtime story. At home, with his mother, even Orry "defaults to English," Adrian admits.

It is why, even in the heart of the revivalist community, anxieties persist. Only time will tell whether the playground's sounds signal a renaissance, or whether they are a 1,500-year-old language's last gasp.

Ten

AN ENGLISHMAN AT
L'ACADÉMIE FRANÇAISE

S ir Michael Edwards, the first and only Englishman at
the French Academy, invited me to a teatime rendez-
vous last summer at his home near Saint-Germain-des-Prés.
The tea, though, never arrived. It was one of those stiflingly
hot Paris days when the thermometer temperature exceeds
one hundred; perhaps the French part of my host's mind
simply didn't consider it to be tea weather. Too polite — too
English — I dared not suggest otherwise. I thought delicious
thoughts about the milky cuppa I did not drink.

No matter. We talked, now in English, now in French, in
the book-filled salon till late in the evening; I had so much
to ask him about. At seventy-seven, Sir Michael's life and
career had been long and rich. A scholar and author of verse
who works in a French he learned as a British schoolboy, he
had become one of the language's forty *Immortels,* its undying defenders and overseers, two years earlier. In the four
hundred years since Cardinal Richelieu dreamed up the

Academy, soldiers and clerics, chemists and numismatists, admirals and hotel-keepers, an African head of state, and—beginning in 1980—even a few women, had all been admitted. But never, before Sir Michael, had an Englishman.

His election made headlines; the French papers were particularly generous. The daily *Liberation* enthused, "England has sent us a beautiful gift." The reaction was different across the Channel, in London. The reporters there did not know quite what to make of the news. A fellow from Blighty refining French's official dictionary! They did little to conceal their surprise. "The academy is famous for its tireless battles against 'Anglo-Saxon' invasions of French, offering Gallic equivalents to Anglicisms, such as *courriel* instead of email," noted the *Telegraph*. Explaining himself to his country's press, Sir Michael said, "This is a moment of crisis for French, and it makes sense, I believe, for the academy to choose someone who comes from, as it were, the opposite camp but has become a champion of the special importance and beauty of the French language." In one of his many interviews for the French media he was reported as saying that his favorite word was *France*.

"Actually, I don't know where that came from," Sir Michael told me. "I remember someone pushing a microphone to my mouth and asking me for my favorite word. My favorite French word, of course. The answer just fell out of me. Come to think of it I much prefer *rossignol* ('nightingale')."

The surprise at his election—and not all of it was British—surprised him. But he could entertain the surprise, up to a point. England and France, after all, had a history. Each, to the other, had once been an invader. Each, against the other, had gone to war. On the fields of Agincourt, thousands from both armies had been turned into arrow fodder. So the brows raised at Sir Michael's ascension to the Academy was, from a historian's point of view, understandable. From a linguist's, however, the surprise was unfounded. *Surprise* — the origin of the word is French. Like *election* and *history* and *armies* and *origin*. According to one estimate, one out of four English words was imported from France: to speak British English is to speak a quarter French. (United States English is another matter. Americans pump their trucks with gas, not with petrol (*pétrole*); cook zucchinis and eggplants, not *courgettes* and *aubergines*; shop at the drugstore, not at the pharmacy (*pharmacie*). Leaf-yellowing autumn (*automne*) in New York or San Diego is fall.)

For Sir Michael, the queen, with whom he had an audience on her 2014 state visit to Paris, symbolizes the close relationship between the two languages. A descendant of William the Conqueror, the monarch (whose motto is *Dieu et mon droit* — "God and my right"), has a reputation for fluency in French. "The Queen always speaks first. She complimented me on my living here: 'A very beautiful city.' That's about as much as I can tell you. Conversations with her Majesty must remain confidential."

On a shelf stood a framed photograph of their meeting.

"Did you converse in English or in French?"

"In English. But at the state banquet later that evening, she spoke in French."

The banquet took place in a chandeliered hall of the Élysée Palace. In the bright lights, the queen, in white, sparkled with diamonds, and the red riband over her right shoulder told all that she belonged to the Legion of Honour. As she spoke, she turned the pages of her speech with white-gloved hands. Banquet etiquette—it is the royal custom to read from notes—but I was curious. What was Sir Michael's opinion of the queen's linguistic performance? Suddenly, predictably, diplomacy came to him. He would only say, "very good." I remembered then that the speech had been televised live in France (the queen is as popular as ever with foreign republicans), as had others she had given in the past, and recordings of them could be watched online. I found several, some days after the meeting with Sir Michael, and listened. No, Sir Michael did not speak the Queen's French. His pronunciation was even better, his accent even smoother. And later still, reading up, I learned that the queen had picked up her second language not in France but within the walls of her father's palace; it turned out to be a by-product of her cloistered upbringing, the work of a Belgian governess—proof, paradoxically, of her unworldliness.

(And, reading further, I came upon a contemporary account of the French spoken by the queen's namesake, Elizabeth I: "She spoke French with purity and elegance, but with a drawling, somewhat affected accent, saying 'Paar maa foi; paar le Dieeu vivaant,' and so forth, in a style that was ridiculed by Parisians, as she sometimes, to her extreme annoyance, discovered.")

Sir Michael—though he now moves in high circles, an

easy converser with queens and presidents and prime ministers — is of humble beginnings and had to learn French the hard way. No Belgian governess for him! "I was born and raised in Barnes, in southwest London. Very English, the pubs and parks and street names: Cromwell Road, Tudor Drive. Modest, too." His father, Frank, a garage owner, worked in car parts. Sir Michael's aspirations were his mother's doing. "As a girl she had written a play. Of course, nothing ever came of it, but it stayed with her, this dream of making a living out of words." Her son was able to cultivate his ambition at an Elizabethan all-boys secondary school, Kingston Grammar. (*Grammar,* another French word, meaning "book learning," is a cousin of *glamour.*) "I fell for French. I was eleven. I opened my textbook — *A Grammar of Present Day French with Exercises,* by J. E. Mansion — and there they were: *oui* and *non.* Such magic in so simple words. *Yes* and *no.* But how important! It was the same with other French words. They possessed an aura." To the garage owner's boy, the words seemed bright and shocking with unfamiliarity. "A new world opened to me: new ways of naming, of seeing, of imagining."

And taking in Sir Michael now, the embroidered red lion on his navy-blue tie, his black leather slippers; looking into the ingratiating eyes behind the metal-rimmed spectacles; attending to his studied clubability, his professorial way of speaking ("Bother," "Vivat!") — so dapper in dress, so clerkish in manner — you can see how the British grammar school, at a remove of sixty-plus years, had laid the foundation for his present role. Had he always enjoyed his school lessons?

"No. I remember finding the textbooks dry, cold, unfriendly. Probably they put off many of my classmates. I was never put off, but then somehow I knew that French was so much better than its textbooks."

He recalled his French schoolmaster. "Dr. Reginald Nicholls. He had a spastic jaw. Quite the disadvantage for a language teacher."

Dry textbooks, a teacher with a spastic jaw—and when, after seven years at Kingston Grammar, Sir Michael went to Cambridge, he was taught French "as though it were dead." All reading, no speaking. Taught only to decipher Montaigne and Voltaire and Racine. Once again, education might have thrown him off French forever. But Racine enchanted. Sir Michael went on to write a thesis in Paris on Racine. And flexing his memory, Sir Michael recited a little Racine to me:

Moi-même, il m'enferma dans des cavernes sombres,
Lieux profonds et voisins de l'empire des ombres.

The citation is from *Phèdre*. And while we were on the subject of the play, Sir Michael said, "French and English writers don't think and write alike. Racine taught me that. For instance, an English author would never write, as Racine does, *à l'ombre des forêts* ("in the shadow of forests"); he would write 'in the shadow of a cedar' or 'in the shadow of an oak tree.'"

"Interesting. So the two languages configure reality differently. Could you tell me a little more about this difference? How would you characterize it?"

"I would say perceptions in French are more abstract — like hovering over an experience in a Montgolfier. It's the reason why French thoughts tend to be holistic, and the texts homogenous. Whereas English perceiving is earthier, detail-led, full of quirks."

"What do you mean by texts that are 'homogenous'?"

"Racine wrote many plays, but he wrote them with few words: two thousand. Shakespeare's contain ten times more. That gives you an idea of how few Racine needed. In French, a same word can be made to say several different things. Consider *attrait* — a typical Racine word. Applied to a woman it means 'charms'; but use it to describe something vaguer, like the unknown, and you have to translate it as 'lure': *l'attrait de l'inconnu,* the lure of the unknown. The 'attractiveness' of a town or city, an 'interest' in some topic, feeling 'drawn' to this or that — all meanings that merge in *attrait*. It's this quality in French that helps a text cohere."

Out of modesty, perhaps, Sir Michael didn't mention Racine's links to the Academy. The subject of Sir Michael's thesis, the author of *Phèdre,* the model of the French language's "purity" and "eloquence" (the terms are Richelieu's), Racine, born less than four years after the Academy, joined its ranks at the age of thirty-three. So in Racine, Sir Michael also has an illustrious predecessor.

Racine took him to Paris. And in Paris he met and later married Danielle, a Frenchwoman. "My children and grandchildren all have French citizenship. I would have become a French citizen myself much sooner had I known that it was possible to keep both nationalities. You see, I didn't want to lose my British passport." With his French wife and British passport, Sir Michael taught French, English, and comparative literature for many years in Warwick, Essex, and Paris (with stints in Belfast, Budapest, and Johannesburg). In addition to his career in academia, he reviewed French and English poetry for the *Times Literary Supplement.*

"I was sent a book of poems by Yves Bonnefoy to review. Later we became firm friends. A quintessentially French author. It was he who gave me the idea to write in the language."

Sir Michael has gone on to write many books, in both languages, including a study of Samuel Beckett, another favorer of French over his native English. In *Paris Aubaine,* a recent verse collection, Sir Michael even mixes the two together, sometimes within the same sentence: "Inspecting her woodcuts, I thought the Seine too sinewy, turmoiled and yet, l'eau grise, sous la haute pierre, s'anime de guivres, se trouble là-bas, dans les remous de sa présence unearthly."

Guivre, a heraldic term for "serpent" (perhaps Sir Michael, composing his verse, had in mind the Serpentine River in London's Hyde Park), was, I thought, just the sort of classical and "quintessentially French" word of which the Academy approved. But *guivre* had, in fact, been given no entry in the first edition of the Academy's dictionary, published in 1694. Lack of space — the work stretched to only 18,000 entries — was one explanation. A likelier explanation could be found in the early academicians' curious attitude toward words.

Claude Favre de Vaugelas, a nobleman whose influence among his colleagues ran high, championed a vocabulary that avoided anything the tiniest bit provincial, vulgar, or technical. Keep French gentlemanly — such could have been his motto. Gentlemen in France had seemlier things to talk about than serpents.

The silliness in the dictionary's making was exceeded only by the slowness. Nitpickers expended weeks on the definition of a word like *bouche* ("mouth"). After fifteen years at the dictionary, Vaugelas and his fellow academicians had only gotten as far as the letter *I*; dying prevented him from reaching *je* or *jovial* or *jupe*. Years later, in a moment of crossness, Antoine Furetière complained about the energies wasted on pointless arguments:

> Right is he who shouts loudest; everyone harangues over the merest trifle. The second man repeats like an echo what the first has just said, and most often they speak three or four at a time. When five or six are present, one will be reading, another opining, two chitchatting, one dozing.... Definitions read aloud have to be repeated because someone wasn't listening.... Not two lines' worth of progress is made without long digressions.

Furetière was also at work on his own dictionary. When the others at the Academy found out, they told him to stop. He refused; he had put the best years of his life — over thirty — into the project. For this refusal he was thrown out.

The subsequent back-and-forth between the Academy and its former member came to be known as "the quarrel of the dictionaries." The Academy's, fifty years in the writing and still incomplete, was a mess. Furetière revealed that many of its entries weren't in alphabetical order; that a word as common as *girafe* ("giraffe") was nowhere to be found; that the arguers could not decide whether to list *a* as a vowel or as a word. That the academicians reduced their dictionary to an exercise in dilettantism was bad enough; their dropping whole parts of the language for being less tasteful than others was to Furetière incredible. "An architect speaks just as good French, talking plinths and stylobates, and a soldier, talking casemates, merlons, and Saracens, as a courtesan who talks alcoves, daises, and chandeliers." Admirers of Furetière published his dictionary (containing an entry for *guivre*) in three volumes in Holland in 1690, two years after his death and four before the Academy at last presented its own, much sparser, to the court of Louis XIV. The Sun King preferred Furetière's.

Furetière's achievement threw into relief the Academy's shortcomings as a dictionary maker. One man had done what scores, over sixty years of fits-and-starts labor, had struggled—and failed—to do. As a parable of individual endeavor—one head better than a hundred—it is compelling. Even more compelling, and embarrassing for the academicians, was the publication in 1755 of the *Dictionary of the English Language,* by Samuel Johnson. "Without any patronage of the great; not in the soft obscurities of retirement, or under the shelter of academic bowers, but amidst inconvenience and distraction, in sickness and in sorrow," Johnson wrote of the seven (some accounts say eight, others nine) years it had taken him to define some forty-two thousand English words. Johnson had had to work fast to pay back the local booksellers whose commission money kept him in ink and paper. The speed had come at the expense of sleep and temper, but not — it was his pride — of quality. Critics, at home and abroad, were impressed. What quill power! Johnson, feigning modesty, called himself English's "humble drudge."

They were the remarks of a man looking back, separate from the past, now at ease in his accomplishment. At the start of his labor, though, Johnson's ambition had been much wilder. Having looked at a copy of the Academy's third edition (published in 1740), his thoughts, like the thoughts of the academicians in Paris, turned to fixing his language, making it exempt from the corruption of workers and foreigners. Johnson's initial aim wasn't, therefore, to record every word employed in England. His dictionary was to be selective; in compliance with his patriotism, the author would leave out many French words, or at least discourage the reader from using them. He didn't want his countrymen to "babble a dialect of France." Of *ruse,* he wrote, "a French word neither elegant nor necessary." *Finesse* he also deemed "an unnecessary word which is creeping into the language." *Spirit* used in the French sense, to mean "a soul" or "a person," was, Johnson added, "happily growing obsolete." Instead of *heroine* he recommended that Britons say and write *heroess.* But in the course of his long toil, Johnson's snobbery softened. Some words were simply too beautiful or too useful to care much about where they came from. Like *paramour,* which Johnson conceded is "not inelegant or unmusical."

Johnson, though he began his dictionary with an academician's cast of mind, closed it with quite another. The very idea of a language needing fixing struck him in the end as nonsense. Academies like the French one, he asserted, could never work: sounds are "too volatile and subtle for legal restraints"; syllables cannot be put in chains, nor speech "lashed" into obedience. "The edicts of an English academy would, probably, be read by many," he noted wryly, "only that they might be sure to disobey them."

The year after his election, Sir Michael was honored with a ceremony welcoming him to the Academy. In keeping with an old tradition, the members attributed to him a word and definition from their dictionary (now on its ninth edition and counting some sixty thousand entries). They chose *universalité:*

> n. f. Ensemble, totalité, ce qui embrasse les différentes espèces. *L'universalité des êtres, des sciences, des arts.* En termes de Jurisprudence, *L'universalité des biens,* La totalité des biens.
>
> UNIVERSALITÉ signifie aussi Caractère de ce qui est universel, de ce qui s'étend à un très grand nombre de pays, d'hommes. *L'universalité de la langue française...*

(In my translation: "a set, a totality, that which subsumes the different kinds. *The universality of beings, of sciences, of arts.* In jurisprudence, *the universality of goods [entirety of assets],* the totality of goods. *Universality* also refers to the condition of that which is universal, of that which extends to a very great number of countries, of people. *The universality of the French language . . .*")

It is on such definitions that Sir Michael and eleven of his colleagues on the dictionary commission work. "Thursday is dictionary day. The twelve of us sit around a long table for three hours in the morning, going through the latest revisions to be debated one by one. It might be a definition that needs tweaking. Or an entry's example that needs replacing. Or a neologism of some sort. We probably get through around twenty or thirty words a week. It sounds like a sinecure, but we take our duties very seriously. The atmosphere in the room is pretty solemn. You have to ask permission to speak." He raised his arm, as if he were looking at the commission's chairman, and lowered it again.

"At the same time there's a camaraderie. All those hours together, we become real buddies, *on se tutoie* [meaning that they address each other with the familiar form of *you* — *tu*]."

The commission was currently scrutinizing the possible meanings of *rude*. Unlike the English *rude*, the French has many uses: it can mean "rough," "unpolished," "unsophisticated," "harsh," and "severe."

"Not long to go before we're finally out of the *R*'s." He smiled. *"Ars longa, vita brevis."* An academician's joke.

It was not only the *R*'s that kept Sir Michael and his colleagues busy. Responsibility for answering usage queries from the public rests with the commission. In the old days, the queries arrived in envelopes and fussy handwriting. Now, they come typed in emails. *Courriel*. Not "e-mail." The commission's answers appear on a dedicated page of the Academy's website. To Edwin S., who inquired whether one should say *Quand est-ce que tu viens?* ("What time do you arrive?") or *Quand viens-tu?,* a commission member replied that the latter was better, even if — it had to be admitted — the former was far more common. A certain Shiraga wrote in to query the French pronunciation of *bonzaï;* in its native Japanese, she remarked, the word is pronounced "bonssai." The French should always pronounce it with a z sound, the commission said, and added sternly "It is not a Japanese word, but a French word that has been borrowed from Japanese."

Sometimes the responder is Sir Michael. He also contributes to the Academy's style guide (published, too, on the website): *Dire, Ne Pas Dire* (*Say, Do Not Say*). According to the guide, for instance, "we don't say" *il est sur la short list* ("he is on the shortlist"); *shortlist,* too English, is out. "We say," instead, *il est parmi les derniers candidats susceptibles d'obtenir tel prix* ("he is among the remaining candidates capable of obtaining such prize"). A roundabout way of putting it, to say the least. And on and on, in the same convoluted vein, the guide goes.

We don't say *une newsletter;* we say *une lettre d'informations.*

We don't say *une single;* we say *une chambre pour une personne.*

We don't say *éco-friendly;* we say *respectueux de l'environnement.*

So many proscriptions! Don't. Don't. Don't. It made for rather unpleasant reading.

But Sir Michael said I had gotten the guide wrong. The guide isn't anti-English. Many in the Academy he called Anglophiles, admirers of British and American novels, the words of Wordsworth and the like. No, he said, it is a matter of clarity. Many English words confuse. The "artificial English," bizarre and stunted, that globalization peddles. On posters in the Paris subway, on billboards near Notre Dame, in loud radio ads that resound along boulevards: *Just do it! Nespresso, What Else? Taste the feeling! This is Her! This is Him!* Sir Michael sees all around him landscapes disfigured by these meaningless slogans. "It is something my colleagues have long and rightly bellyached about. The health of a nation," he said, as if reciting, "depends on the health of its language."

Thus the aesthetic defense of French has given way to the ethical. No longer is the Academy protecting French for gentlemen; it is preserving French for the common man. But behind the ethical posture, as behind the aesthetic, the same anxieties, the same obsessions. A kind of language panic. In 1985 in a public speech to the Academy, Sir Michael's predecessor, the author Jean Dutourd, denounced "the murder of syntax, the genocide of the dictionary" being committed by the boorish purveyors of "Atlantic pidgin." They had the "rapacity of real estate developers," Dutourd warned, who, given half a chance, would demolish the "palace" of the French language to build a super-luxury high-rise over it. He wanted the French government to take action. He told his genteel audience he wanted to see a "linguistic inquisition" in France. He urged the finance minister to create a grammar inspectorate whose task would be to comb the press, books, and ads for bastardized words. Anyone who published *nominer* ("to nominate") instead of *nommer* (the older French form), or who, under the influence of English, mixed up *sanctuaire* and *refuge,* would have to pay a fine of twenty francs. A tax on words!

Admittedly, Sir Michael is no Jean Dutourd (whose books, before coming to the Academy, Sir Michael had never read). He is a moderate. He does not believe in taxing words. Like the Academy's website, his moderation is a concession to the twenty-first century. "French is changing, France is changing. I'm part of the changing face of France." Behind his gray head, the frilly orange-red lampshade was distracting. "Of course the language needs to be fixed to some extent, to remain readable one hundred years from now," he continued, "but we mustn't try to stop the future" ("We mustn't be Jean Dutourds," he could have said). "Can we really expect any human institution not to have its share of boring old farts?"

"We mustn't try to stop the future." But I couldn't be sure Sir Michael meant that. I couldn't understand why the Academy considers, for example, *jazzman* and *blackout* and *fair play* and *covergirl* all acceptable French words, but thinks *shortlist* too English, or degenerate English. *Blackout* turns up in several novels by Patrick Modiano, winner of the

2014 Nobel Prize in Literature. J. M. G. Le Clézio, France's other living Nobel laureate (he won in 2008), uses *covergirl* in his novel *Désert*. What is to stop either of them writing *shortlist* into a future work of French literature? Certainly not the Academy's style guide. Neither writer—I note in passing—has shown any interest in joining the Academy.

It was getting on—with all the talking, we had forgotten about the clock—but before leaving Sir Michael, I asked to see the famous books and rooms at the Institut de France that he and his fellow academicians use during their conclaves. He said that could be arranged. The Academy would sit again in the autumn; I should send him a reminder then.

I did. And Sir Michael was as good as his word. After summering in Burgundy, he replied with a date, Thursday, November 12, and an address, 23 quai de Conti. (The assembly's address was superfluous. My apartment was little more than a stone's throw away: I walked past the pillared façade every time I crossed the Pont des Arts.) On the twelfth, at an hour when the afternoon *séance* was winding up, I presented myself to the young lady at the reception. I said I was there to see "Michael Edwards." The receptionist looked blank. I tried again. I said, pronouncing his name as if it were a Frenchman's, "Michelle Edooar."

"Ah, Monsieur Edooar!" She handed me a security badge, let me through the electronic turnstiles, told me where to go to sit and wait.

Across the cobbled courtyard was the door, closed, forbidding.

I tried the door. It creaked, then opened. Busts, tapestries, chandeliers. Presently Sir Michael came down a staircase. The setting's pomposity stiffened his gait. The academicians had been "inside" for their weekly one-and-a-half-hour plenary session, he explained, during which the dictionary commission's suggestions were mooted. Thursday afternoons at the Academy often went smoothly, but this one had been more difficult. He was about to tell me more, but apparently thought better of it. He changed the subject. "Let me show you the library."

The Mazarin library: the seat of French letters. Six hundred thousand volumes wall to wall. Here, amid the smell of vellum, musty leather, and millions of pages steeped in centuries, Sir Michael's 1965 thesis on Racine rubbed covers with the original plays; with a 1580 copy of John Baret's *Alvearie*, a multilingual dictionary—English, Latin, French, and a sprinkling of Greek—"newlie enriched with varietie of wordes, phrases, proverbs, and divers lightsome observations of grammar," which Shakespeare, in composing his own plays, is thought to have consulted; with *Notre Dame de Paris*, by Victor Hugo, who became an Academy member only after being turned down thrice; with the collected poems of Baudelaire, whose sole candidacy, in 1862, went nowhere.

Sir Michael said, "I believe that's because he'd had a run-in with the law." The Academy had also rejected Molière (whose name has become forever associated with French: *la langue de Molière*), Pascal, and Zola at one time or another.

About his own candidacy, Sir Michael said, "You hand-write a letter to each academician. And each letter has to be personalized. You're advised not to write too much. I may have gone over to a second page." He admitted to having been unfamiliar with the names of several of the academicians; he'd had to mug up the titles of their books, their themes, and their styles beforehand.

Walking me through long corridors from the library to the Academy's assembly room, Sir Michael showed me a statue of Jean de La Fontaine, beside which, on his first day, as the "new boy," he had been made to wait until called. Inside the stuffy assembly room, below the gilded portrait of Richelieu, forty plush red seats were laid out in an oval. Each academician's seat is numbered. Sir Michael's is Seat 31. Cocteau once sat there, as did the author of *Cyrano de Bergerac,* Edmond Rostand.

It was here, one Thursday afternoon, in seat 29, that the anthropologist Claude Lévi-Strauss gave his definition of *boomerang.* And it was here, on another Thursday afternoon, that Lévi-Strauss persuaded his colleagues to modify the dictionary's entry for *rance* ("rancid"). According to him, the entry, which spoke of a "disagreeable" taste and odor, betrayed a Western bias. For many cultures, he told the room, rancidity is part and parcel of their cuisine. His complaint was upheld: *disagreeable* was cut and replaced with *strong.*

I wondered whether Sir Michael would also leave a mark on the Academy's dictionary. I wondered whether he would speak up, out of his Englishness, when the time came for the assembly to look again at *sandwich,* say, or *turf.*

He read my thoughts. Or perhaps his being back in the place where, only an hour or two before, emotions had flared and words had been crossed, moved him to recount.

"I suppose I bring to the Academy a way of speaking that's a bit different. I'm not above making a joke. At the same time I'm not afraid to speak my mind. I have opinions." He stopped, looked around, lowered his voice and said in a confiding tone, "I had a bit of a dingdong with Giscard." Giscard is Valéry Giscard d'Estaing, nearly ninety, president of France between 1974 and 1981; he was elected to the Academy in 2003. The Englishman's and ex-president's dingdong was over how to sum up *vamp.* "He started it. He claimed it means *une belle séductrice.* Pure and simple. I said 'No, it means more than that.' I said it came from *vampire,* and therefore suggests a dangerousness alongside the beauty." Apparently much of the session was taken up with their dispute.

The French penchant for abstract, never-ending debate! After ten years living in France, I know it well. Frenchmen and Frenchwomen, it is widely said, pay little attention to the Academy, and in my experience they don't have to. A family lunch, lasting hours, is their academy. Sharing a wine with friends on a noisy bistro terrace is their academy. How the French love to talk! And to talk about talk!

Back at the reception the lady helped Sir Michael into his long black Burberry coat. He was off to a Schubert concert; he is an inveterate concertgoer. "Our annual meeting is in three weeks' time. All the academicians will be there. Dressed up in our uniforms, you know, like a bunch of deposed South American junta generals. I'll see you're invited. I'll be presiding."

The following evening, Friday, November 13, 2015, two miles from the Academy and my home, one hundred and thirty rockers, bistro diners, and café drinkers were killed in a coordinated attack by radical Islamist terrorists. Hundreds more were wounded. A state of emergency was declared.

Violence has a way of reducing the mundane to a pure ridiculousness. Already it had been hard enough to begin to write about the French Academy — its quaint rituals and pointless-sounding arguments — without making it sound absurd. Now 130 deaths. In comparison with them, what did it matter how a dictionary defined *vamp?*

But the more I thought about the violence — so ruthless, so flagrant, designed to wow and whet hatred — the less absurd the Academy, its work, its role, began to seem. Violence levels everything, turns bricks, bottles, and bodies indiscriminately into so much rubbish. The academicians, contrariwise, seek to discern, weigh, conserve. Violence silences; the Academy champions words. *La mort injuste* versus *le mot juste*.

President Obama, offering American condolences, reached for French words: "The American people draw strength from the French people's commitment to life, liberty, the

pursuit of happiness. We are reminded in this time of trag-
edy that the bonds of *liberté* and *égalité* and *fraternité* are not
only values that the French people care so deeply about, but
they are values that we share."

And in the days after the attacks, throughout Paris, a
book originally written in English, by an American, sold by
the thousands: Hemingway's *A Moveable Feast*.

Once again, hearteningly, that close relationship between
the two languages.

Three weeks later, with my invitation card, I waited in
line at 23 quai de Conti before passing security. December's
Academy was more austere in the chill air. Men in Swiss
guard–like costume, all white gloves and red feathers,
clanked to attention as we filed inside. We sat under the
cupola—a building set aside for such grand occasions—
concentrically. In the audience, French household names: a
singer, a filmmaker, a telegenic author. And the capital's
bourgeoisie.

Solemnly, the academicians came in and sat together.
Each wore a green and black waistcoat, bicorn hat, cape,
and épée. They were very white, very old, very male. (About
the Academy's woman problem Sir Michael had told me,
"The Academy falls over backwards to elect women; we
want women; not enough women apply.") Sir Michael asked
for a minute's silence in memory of the victims.

After the silence, after the applause for the winners of the
Academy's literary prizes, after a speech on the history of
the French novel, Sir Michael cleared his throat and spoke.
He spoke of violence. Not the violence of gunmen—the

type, exercised by poets, (in my translation) "against conventional perspectives on life and self, against tired clichés." But the poet's violence, Sir Michael continued, was that of someone who "cracks a nut, or bites into a fruit." A "violence of the poetic act," which is always accompanied by "gentleness in the respect for the real."

Reality, he concluded, responds to language. "Reality," he had told me, months before, in his apartment, "is polyglot."

Eleven

OULIPO

Pity who, as typist, in 1969, had to turn a famous Parisian author's fourth manuscript into book form: *La Disparition* (*A Vanishing* or *A Void*). Our typist sits at his contraption and, palms cast customarily downward, starts jabbing away; but rhythm is hard to find. Fit digits, usually busy, now look to him lazy or numb. Tsk-tsking this or that digit won't do him any good, though. It's all about using his hands unorthodoxly. It's all about application, knuckling down. His right pinky works, his right thumb works. Clack, clack, clack...ding. Clack, clack, clack...ding. But application or no application, typos abound; a hand has its habits. So our struggling typist starts again, and again, until paragraphs, long and looping, catalogs of copious food and drink, slapstick situations, parodic imitations of Arthur Rimbaud and Victor Hugo, comic accounts of killings, sixty thousand–plus words total, finally all turn out without a slip—without so much as a whiff of *français*'s most common symbol twixt *d* and *f*.

A short illustration:

Anton Voyl n'arrivait pas à dormir. Il alluma. Son Jaz marquait minuit vingt. Il poussa un profond soupir, s'assit dans son lit, s'appuyant sur son polochon. Il prit un roman, il l'ouvrit, il lut; mais il n'y saisissait qu'un imbroglio confus, il butait à tout instant sur un mot dont il ignorait la signification.

(In my translation: "Anton Vowl couldn't drift off. On had to go his lamp. His *Jaz* alarm clock told him it was past midnight. With much sighing Vowl sat up in his pajamas, his pillow for a prop. Took a book to dip into; but saw in it only an imbroglio of ink, fumbling to grasp this or that word's signification.")

La Disparition's author was "Gargas Parac"* (an alias of his making). Born in 1936, an orphan at six (his *papa* and *maman* both victims of Nazism), Parac was a sociologist by training—working in public opinion polls and as an archivist/information coordinator until his skillful and ambitious writing paid off. A first book, *Things,* was brought out in 1965 and won him instant standing and a major *prix.* But it was his falling in with OuLiPo (an acronym that roughly stands for "workshop for writing within constraints"), a multinational group of *avant*-guard authors, that would prod his imagination to think about words and grammar in a surprisingly original fashion.

(Also in OuLiPo: Italo Calvino, writing in Italian, author of *Cosmicomics* (with, for narrator, Qfwfq), *Mr. Palomar,* and

---

* Editor's Note: With the fifth letter of the alphabet in play, the pseudonym is, of course, Georges Perec's.

his *Città Invisibili,* in which Marco Polo and Kublai Khan discuss Polo's distant and fantastic sojourns.)

Writing within constraints: for Parac, as for Calvino, it was an opportunity to pull back from linguistic norms and so avoid stock ways of using words. Parac's boundary was lipogrammatic: truncating his ABCs by a most popular symbol, and sifting through his vocabulary to pick out all words containing it. Up to two thirds of quotidian *français* was thus out of bounds for his forthcoming book. Just thinking of writing within such limits might throw many of us into a panic. But for Parac it was a stimulant to lift him out of his chronic author's block.

Lipograms had a long history, dating back to antiquity. Lasus of Argolis, writing around 500 BC, known primarily for his dithyrambs and for tutoring Pindar, was also an originator of hymns minus any sigma (*s*): its hissing sound grating on him. Lasus wasn't a 1-off. At Romanticism's high point, a Gottlob Burmann (1737–1805) of dainty constitution brought out an opus of soft-sounding lyrics that contain no harsh *r*: no *Frau,* no *dürr* ("thin"), no *rann* ("ran").

In Paris, Parac's lipogrammatic writing was a first. Its author had at his disposal a total of 25 ABC symbols, originating in Latin, not all individually so old. Copyist monks in Norman scriptoria had had no *j* or *v*: quills would put down *iour* for *jour* ("day"), *auait* for *avait* ("had"); it wasn't until 1762 that *j* was always told apart from *i,* and *u* from *v. W,* though known to Walloons, did not gain a national dictionary's sanction until 1964.

So Parac had *w* to put in writing (a joy to him, having a soft spot for it), *j* and *v, s*'s that Lasus did without, and *r,* which

Burmann was always avoiding. But not what a schoolchild is normally taught to jot down—along with *a, i, o,* and *u*—whilst still small. Not what looks much as a mirror's portrait of a 3. A most difficult taboo to work around: statistically it amounts to 1 in 7 ABC symbols in a Gallic book (by way of comparison, 1 in 8 in a Californian or British opus, 1 in 6 in Dutch). Our author had his work cut out for him.

As a backdrop to his writing, Parac had Paris's May 1968 riots: a capital in turmoil, young anarchists occupying public buildings, shouting slogans, scrawling graffiti against an out-of-touch administration. Orthographic acts of fury. No to *flics* (cops)! No to *intox*—short for *intoxication* (propaganda)! Plays on words, on symbols. An infamous placard said all it had to say succinctly, in just a handful of symbols: *CRS SS* (*CRS* is an acronym standing for *riot control units*). Thus, a community's *a*'s and *s*'s and *x*'s and so on could impart information in print, could signify, without always participating in a word. A word wasn't simply a unitary transcription of sounds; its constituting symbols (*f-l-i-c-s, i-n-t-o-x,* groupings as familiar as "*c-r-s—s-s*") also had things to say. This was Parac's crucial insight—his bolt of brain lightning.

Part artistic, part political, our wordsmith's goal was to show how important ABC layout is in how words in a book, a tract, a tabloid, a glossy, "talk" to us and "think" for us. Linguists call this *visual iconicity*: symbols composing a word mimic, up to a point, what it talks about. Iconicity, at its most basic, says that short words using an ABC's most popular symbols—such as *rash* (*r-a-s-h*)—will, broadly, bring up day-to-day things; long words that consist of

uncommon symbols or unusual combinations of symbols—
such as *psoriasis* (*p-s-o-r-i-a-s-i-s*)—discuss knotty, atypical
affairs. In addition, symbols' forms in union can act as a
visual aid, portraying a word's topic. By way of illustration,
think of *locomotion*. Its *l* is a pictorial fuming puff; its consonants, wagons; and its four *o*'s, what roll on rails. Similarly,
Victor Hugo thought *lys* ("lily") a right orthographic form
and its rival *lis* wrong. For *y* to his mind was akin to a sprig
with consonants as blossoms surrounding it.

Browsing *La Disparition*, taking in its paragraphs, a striking thing is its fair lack of diacritic marks. So far as "hats" on
nouns go, only a small quantity show up: *août* ("August"),
trouvât ("found"), *chaînon* ("link in a chain"). It turns out
that as soon as you start amputating all words containing
français's fifth ABC symbol, you must also lock out much
vocabulary that is put down diacritically. To purists, Parac's
book, its words' physiognomy, is an optical shock. Almost an
insult. A "hat" on a noun—an offshoot of *Orthographia Gal-
lica* (composition around 1300)—boasts symbolic status
today. It's a bit posh. It's why folk who want to climb a social
rung will occasionally add a "hat" to nouns that don't don it,
putting down, say, *ajoût* ("addition"); on all occasions it is
right to put *ajout*. It's why a 1990 commission's proposal to
simplify orthography by dropping *français*'s surplus "hats"
got swiftly told off by columnists and public outcry.

(Occasionally an ABC symbol can amount in authors'
minds not to a plus but to a stigma: in Russia, around 1900,
writings by anti-tsar radicals would fashionably omit from
nouns Cyrillic's "hard sign," [*tvyordy znak*]—a ъ that marks

a word's final consonant as non-palatal — associating it with backward-looking ritual.)

La Disparition is a zany whodunit, a curious story about abyss and oblivion, in which a man, Anton Voyl, fights awful insomnia. "Why amn't I dozing?" Voyl asks. Doctors can only shrug. Psychopharmacologists' pills do not work. Gradually, Voyl and a fair many of his pals drop out of sight, go missing, vanish into thin air. Victims of booby traps? Shootings? Stabbings? Falling pianos? A mafia's hitlist? In hot pursuit, kith and kin toil to find a solution. Parac was a fan of Franz Kafka, and it shows. Mortality is a constant, as in *Richard III*:

> *I had a Richard too, and thou didst kill him;*
> *I had a Rutland too, thou holp'st to kill him.*

An odd mood draws you in, a combination of story and orthography. It's a story told in 25 parts (jumping straight from Part Four to Part Six); a taboo symbol throughout, conspicuous in its omission. Parac, handling his biro with brio, pulls it all off.

I watch an old black-and-gray TV program on which Parac, chubby, a dark billow of curly hair atop his brow, is stating that his story is auto-organizing associations of ABC symbols. His book is its own author, a product of an "automatization of writing." His collocutor and host, going off script, gasps quickly to his public watching, "I should add that this isn't a *canular* ['hoax']."

Automatization of writing? But it is not only promotional tour talk. Think about it. By putting his mind primarily to symbols — not words or plot — Parac was following an original driving logic. Grammar is occasionally his own: a man's brain hurts with *"un fort migrain"*; folks talk with *"cordons vocaux"* ("vocal ribbons"), not vocal cords. If a word such as *lip* is out of bounds in *français*—damn taboo's fault!—our author puts down *"pli labial"* ("labial fold"). Lists push his story forward: *"son minois rubicond, mafflu, lippu, joufflu, bouffi"* ("his rubicund mug, ruddy, lippy, chubby, puffy"). Syntax also adjusts: a first paragraph, a following paragraph, a third, all start with, *"oui, mais"* (*"oui,* but"').

"Portons dix bons whiskys à l'avocat goujat qui fumait au zoo." This postscript in Anton Voyl's diary is also a pangram (a "Parac" pangram, that is, containing 25 ABC symbols out of 26). A variant in *anglais* might go, "a quick brainy fox jumps with a guava lizard."

Parac also plays with words put in print by past virtuosos. Full lipogrammatic modifications of ballads, cantos, stanzas. To supply a notion of how this turns out, my adaptation of "Daffodils," by William Wordsworth:

I, solitary as a cloud
That floats on high past coombs and hills,
Without a warning saw a crowd
A host, of brilliant daffodils;
Along a pool, among hawthorns
Flapping and dancing in mid-morn.

Continuous as bright stars that glow
And glint-glint on our Milky Way,
Ranging in an undying row

Along a margin of a bay:
Six thousand saw I in a flash
Tossing gold crowns in sprightly thrash.

Vivid pool, but my daffodils
Outdid its sparkling in spirit:
A rhymist could not but turn gay
In such a jocund company:
I rapt — so rapt — but hardly thought
What fund this show to us had brought:

For oft, if on my couch I sigh
In vacant or in gray humor,
Gold will flash on that inward mind
Bliss of my on-my-own hours;
And so my soul with passion fills
And frolics with my daffodils.

From paragraph to paragraph throughout his book, always omitting what is twixt *d* and *f,* Parac brings in words from many lands. Thus crop up words in Latin: *oppidum civium romanorum* and *sic transit Gloria Mundi*; words in Italian: *Ah, Padron, siam tutti morti*; USA words: *It is not a gossipy yarn; nor is it a dry, monotonous account, full of such customary fill-ins as "romantic moonlight casting murky shadows down a long, winding country road"*; and "Saarland patois": *man sagt dir, komm doch mal ins Landhaus. Man sagt dir, Stadtvolk muss aufs Land, muss zurück zut Natur. Man sagt dir, komm bald, möglichst am Sonntag.* Truly, *La Disparition* is a multilingual work.

Today, translations of Parac's book sit on racks all around our world: in a city such as Hamburg (*Anton Voyls Forgang*), in Italy (*La Scomparsa*), in Croatia, Holland, and Romania. In Spain it contains no *a* (*a* is Spanish's most common ABC symbol); in Japan, no *i*; in Russia, no *o*. Translations in many lingos; who knows, a stalwart translator may soon put it into South India's Malayalam.

Today, too, computational analysis of *La Disparition*'s prolixity throws up fascinating linguistic data. Word clouds highlight its most-occurring nontrivial vocabulary: *sans* ("without"); *savoir* ("to know"); *grand* ("big") — most words for talking about small things contain Parac's taboo symbol. Also common: *mort* ("dying"); *mot* ("word"); *blanc* ("blank"); *noir* ("black"); *nuit* ("night"); *obscur* ("dim"). Statistical analysis also shows that, for all its innovation, Parac's book strictly follows Zipf's law (found by a Harvard corpus linguist, G. K. Zipf — it was said that if you bought him a Floribunda, G. K. would promptly count all its thorns). Zipf, probing and tallying a library's worth of words, found that in any book roughly half its total vocabulary will occur on only 1 occasion; a book's bulk consists of a handful of its most common words. According to my back-of-a-napkin calculations, *La Disparition* has a vocabulary of around 8,000. A tiny fraction, its 100 most occurring words, crop up so continually as to fill about half of its manuscript; just 400 of its most common words occupy four fifths. Thousands of its words occur only sporadically, turning up on just two occasions throughout Parac's publication; four thousand pop up on just 1.

Including:

Alunir ("to land on a moon"); *axolotl* (a Nahuatl word for a tropical amphibian); *finlandais* ("Finnish"); *hot-dog; infarcti* (plural of *infarction*), *opoponax* (a kind of myrrh — also, a 1964 story by "Monica" Wittig, told with unusual childish narration); *pawlonias* ("Paulownias"); *roucoulant* ("cooing"); *taratata* (a cry of doubt); *uxorilocal* (a social anthropological word for a man living in proximity to his missus's clan).

(Warning: a quantity of Parac's 1-off words, such as *s'anudissant* — "discarding all your clothing" — you won't track down in any standard dictionary.)

And looking again at *La Disparition,* as if with a magnifying glass, past its words, to its individual ABC symbols, you find Zipf's law is also at work. Most of its words contain *a*'s and *i*'s and *n*'s and *u*'s and *s*'s; not many contain *w*'s, *z*'s, *k*'s, *x*'s, or *j*'s. O, it turns out, gains most from Parac's bold plan: *o* round as a nought, a fitting symbol for omission.

If Parac (d. 1982, at 45, of a lung tumor) was still with us, h'd b a fn of txt msging. Not paying a thought to alarmist spoilsports who call it "sad shorthand," "dumbing down," or a "digital virus." No. To him, just gr8 2 play with ltrs in this way, making word drawings such as *bisouXXXXX* (a common nding to a Frnch txt msg, similar to *kixx* for "kiss kiss") and wOw!, was^? ("what's up?"), and "i'm off 2 bd zzzz."

An ABC is a living, fluid, multivocal thing.

Twelve

TALKING HANDS

Visiting a château outside Paris last Christmas, I stepped from a fire-warmed room to find the corridor in commotion. A cascade of kids, in frilly blue and green costumes, came rumbling and tumbling down the stone-slab stairs. On a festive club outing of some kind, the girls and boys in their fancy dress radiated excitement. There was the clack of their heels hurriedly meeting each step, the slap of little palms against thick walls, and the froufrou of flappy outfits as they raced and tussled good-naturedly. And inter-mingled with all of that, something like the burble of collec-tive physical presence, of many simultaneous intakes and outtakes of breath. "They can be *so* noisy," muttered a middle-aged woman beside me. Yet among the group not a word was spoken. Not one shout or shriek. Then it dawned on me that they were deaf children; and, later, on my way out, passing through the grounds in the wintry gloom, I crossed them again, huddled now with their caregivers beneath a street lamp, their busy fingers conversing.

La langue des signes française, the children's sign language — for it most definitely is a language, complete with syntax and morphology and slang—is one of many: every continent has its own distinct forms. But France can claim sign language as England claims English (that more famous global export). A Frenchman, Laurent Clerc, was instrumental in the creation of America's first school for the deaf, in Hartford, Connecticut, in 1817. The system of gestures and facial expressions Clerc brought to the United States had been learned as a boy in Paris, according to methods devised by one Abbot de l'Épée in the mid-1700s. In Yankee hands, the result would become ASL, American Sign Language, which in turn fed several of the forms used widely today across Africa and Asia. So it was that the French, they of the Gallic shrug, as famous as their Italian cousins for the expressivity of their bodies, taught the world to sign.

ASL's quirks, with their roots in the games and garments, the duels and ideas of eighteenth-century France, can mystify the observer. Why do the signs for *tomorrow* (literally, "one [day] into the future") and *yesterday* (literally, "one [day] into the past") enlist the thumb? Because the French count *one* on the thumb and not, as do Americans, on the index. The thumb that flicks out from under the chin to mean *not* in ASL, is the French child's still-popular signal of defiance. *Cannot,* the right index striking down against the left, mimics the sort of swordfights of which Europe's noblemen were once so fond. And if you rightly see a reference to the head in *government*—in which the index lands on the signer's temple—it is only half an explanation: the hand carrying the index first rotates, perhaps drawing the revolutionaries' tricolor cockade.

I was in Montreal, then in Ottawa to see family, some months after that château visit; and, since my aunt spoke French and would have seen deaf patients during her many years at the local hospital's rehabilitation service, I shared my interest in ASL's origins with her. I had even prepared an anecdote (which Emily Shaw and Yves Delaporte recount in one of their *Sign Language Studies* papers), of American commentators interpreting *stupid*—the peace or "V" sign raised to the forehead—all wrong; they claim it represents prison bars that curtail the mind. The gesture, in fact, emulates horns and for a very good French reason: *bête* can mean "stupid" but also "beast."

I never did get round to telling my aunt, Margo Flah, the anecdote. I did not need to. In her youth, she said, she had learned to sign ASL conversations while working at U.S. centers for the deaf. On moving to Canada, she could be seen signing the evening news on television. Car crashes and parliamentary speeches and lottery millions passed through her fingers. People would come up to her in the street. It was a whole side of her I had never known.

Margo offered to teach me the signs of the alphabet. She sat me opposite her at one end of the long table in the living room; and, following her lead, I closed the fingers of my left hand flat over the palm. "*A,*" she said. Then my hand, mirroring hers, contorted into a *B,* a *C,* a *D,* an *E,* an *F.* "Wait!" She broke off. "Are you left-handed?" ASL users, she told me, normally sign with their dominant hand. I write right-handedly, but for some reason, have always thrown with my left. So the choice of hand seemed to depend on the nature of signs: were they something like objects that you pitch through the air, or more like calligraphy, with the space around your body for paper and your hand and arm for brush? I decided to switch to my writing hand. Margo looked relieved. She continued, letter by letter, on through the Zorro-like flourish of Z. Her kindness, her patience, made an enthusiastic student of me. Several times, we ran through the gamut and lingered over those letters my hand did not get quite right. How sharp the practiced signer's eye is! Fingers a fraction too low over the bent thumb formed an inadequate *E*. The fist of *S* needed to be a little tighter. Too much bending of the index spoiled the *X*. Once or twice, leaning over the table, Margo took my hand in hers and gently adjusted my fingers as though setting the time on a slow watch.

"I have two friends you should really meet," Margo said after we had finished signing the alphabet. She invited them round to the house, some mornings later, for coffee and cake.

Notwithstanding his French name, Michel David was raised in an English-speaking Ottawa household. He was a bright-eyed man in his early sixties. He wore Russian green trousers, a checkered shirt beneath a beige sweater, a trim white beard, and, in his left ear, a cochlear implant device.

Monica Elaine Campbell, a few years younger than Michel, was tanned and stylish in a blue-and-white silk scarf, matching blouse, and denim skirt. Her wrists jangled with bracelets, and on the fingers of both hands she had several gold rings. Unlike Michel with his device, she could not hear. She read my lips when I spoke.

We sat around the plate-laden table, in a warm smell of brewing coffee—Michel and Monica Elaine side by side, facing me, with their backs to the window and the bright April sun. Such preliminaries assured Monica Elaine adequate light to see every movement my face and mouth made. Carefully, without hurry, I articulated my words, first of introduction, then of questions for them; in response, Michel and Monica Elaine used ASL (the prevailing sign language in Anglophone Canada) and spoken English.

Michel said, "I'm small-*d* deaf," meaning he did not consider himself culturally deaf; he did not have ASL as his first language. Hearing loss ran in the family, though. As a small boy sitting in the kitchen, he saw his grandmother's cousin communicate in gestures. Around the same time, he noticed that he had a toddler's sense of balance; he had to gaze at a fixed point in the distance as he approached it in order to keep himself plumb. (At night, the lights out, if he ventures to the bathroom without his device he says he stumbles along the landing "like a drunk.") He lay in bed for hours and felt his ears ache. At nine, it seemed to him his parents were always stepping out of his earshot. Forty-decibel loss, the audiologist told them. And that was only the beginning. The son's earshot grew narrower and narrower by the year. Voices, even the loudest, even the most familiar, became patchworks of guesses and memory. In his teens, he turned to ASL; he attended evening classes. Then, one afternoon, while cutting his parents' grass, he heard his ears pop and then nothing. "I thought the mower had died on me." He was twenty. It was the beginning of thirty years in total deafness.

Michel's face was turned toward Monica Elaine as he spoke. She watched his brisk, fluent signs; read the accompanying expressions on his face; and, when he had finished, nodded at the gesture for her to begin. To take a turn. The pouring of pepping coffee, the slicing of aromatic cake, were understandably distracting; and it is considered rude, Michel added, to sign with your hands full.

Monica Elaine was prelingually deaf: her deafness had been discovered at fifteen months. But her parents did not want their daughter to acquire sign language — that would have meant either having to learn ASL as a family or else packing the infant off to a distant school for signing children, and neither option seemed acceptable. So Monica Elaine stayed put with her hearing siblings — three brothers and one sister (a future teacher of the deaf in the United States) — amid the picturesque quays and harbors of Charlottetown, Prince Edward Island.

Presently a new school opened on the island, a school for the lip-reading and speaking deaf. Monica Elaine's parents took the John Tracy Clinic correspondence course to prepare to send their daughter there. They acted on advice from Los Angeles (Spencer Tracy, John's father, was the clinic's main benefactor). The advice was straightforward enough: speak to your deaf child in slow, complete sentences; include her in the everyday life of the family; treat her like any other inquisitive little girl. They followed these principles to the letter, making Monica Elaine fully "speech ready" for when school started. When she was four, it did. In front of a mirror she was taught to form letters in her mouth: the *p* on the lips, the *t* by raising the tip of her tongue to the palate, the *h* by misting the glass with her exhaled breath. Touch — a nervous hand raised to the teacher's cheek and throat — communicated good pronunciation. Little by little the pupil acquired her soft, measured voice.

Monica Elaine's voice is pleasant, easy to understand. Rare are the occasions when she drops a sound from a word ("migle" instead of *mingle*), or replaces one for another ("cazier" for *cashier*). And yet behind the ease lay much personal pain. Growing up, she felt herself "teetering between two worlds," unsure of her identity. Her childhood confusion turned to an adult's anger at not being on signing terms with so many of her peers. Deeply she regretted that her brain had been made to resemble that of a hearing person's. One day, she resolved to study ASL. Never too late to learn. She was thirty-seven.

What courage and perseverance! And it became clear as the morning went on how hard Michel and Monica Elaine had had to fight to lead full lives. They grew up at a time when the attention given to deaf adults' talents and aptitudes was small. Both had nonetheless found in themselves sufficient reserves of determination and self-belief to earn degrees and launch careers.

Michel: "People saw me as a gardener. I had a diploma in horticulture. But then I thought, wait, I can do more. I have a mind. I remembered reading a James Michener novel, *The Source*. The story opens on an archaeological dig in Israel. I got the dollars together and flew to Tel Aviv. I was twenty-one. I spent three months on a kibbutz. Then I took a boat to Cyprus and Greece. I hitchhiked everywhere: through what was then Yugoslavia, Austria, Germany, France, Belgium, Holland. When I was done with Europe, I flew with a Soviet carrier to Japan. I was there several months."

"Did you use sign language with your hosts?"

"Yes. That's the great thing about signing, wherever you are you can usually make yourself understood. And I found foreigners in general to be much more patient with a deaf person."

The experience emboldened him to pursue academic studies on his return home. "The hardest course for me was French. I was forever mixing up the meanings of *entendre* and *comprendre*." After a bachelor's degree in psychology, he moved to Toronto to obtain a master's in social work, started a support group for deaf adults there in 1986, and later became a mental health counselor with the Canadian Hearing Society.

Monica Elaine: "The professors at my university would sometimes walk up and down as they gave their lectures, which made it impossible to lip-read what they were saying." During one of these, the professor spoke for two hours, pacing up and down before garish striped wallpaper: the "visual noise" was uncomfortably loud. And yet she persevered. Mathematics and biology, "very visible subjects," allowed her to play to her strengths. She went on to a long career in human resources.

"At around the time I learned to sign I became involved in palliative care for the deaf." Too ill to write, many deaf patients were deprived of the comfort of communicating with family and friends. She went from hospital to hospital, from deathbed to deathbed, interpreting patients' last signs, reading bloodless lips. For this, in February 2016, Monica Elaine was invested into the Order of Ontario, the province's highest civilian honor.

Michel and Monica Elaine had something else in common, I learned. Their respective partners are hearing. Communication within the couples consists of a mix of speech and signs. Michel is a father of five: all are native signers. "Their first sign, at around ten months, is 'milk.'" He clenched his fist. "Like this. Like pulling an udder. They use it to mean 'food.' They point to milk, crackers, juice and use the same sign. It goes to show how early signing babies can generalize and develop concepts."

Michel had his cochlear implant operation twelve years ago, at 49. His life changed. "My daughter Jessica was three. What a joy to hear her crying!"

He could jump at a clap of thunder, thrill at classical music, or savor the quiet of deaf meetings. But the implant, he acknowledged, is considered a threat in many quarters of the culturally deaf—the big-D Deaf—community. Some fret that it encroaches on their way of life, threatens Deaf pride, undermines the use of sign. Michel, though, did not think in terms of either/or. He considered himself multilingual. He knew the Deaf culture (as did Monica Elaine), for which he had respect. "They are very honest. Honest to the point of bluntness. If you have put on weight since they last saw you, they will sign that you look fatter. At the same time, they won't come right out with their problems. They will tell them within a story."

And Michel and Monica Elaine could understand the Deaf community's vigilance, its desire to cherish all that made sign language so distinctive.

Monica Elaine said, "For instance, to say something like, 'have you ever been to New York?' you use the signs for *New York, touch, finish,* and *question.*"

She signed them for me. To express *question,* the signer's index bends and points in the direction of the person being asked. The upper body also leans forward. ASL grammar, Monica Elaine continued, expanding, is spatial. For instance, leaning forward can also mean the signer is describing something that will happen; likewise, leaning back can indicate that the talk is of what is already in the past. If the signer leans a little to the right (assuming the signer is right-handed), the other person knows that whatever is being signed about occurred only a matter of minutes ago.

One hour conversing with Monica Elaine and Michel grew into two, then three. We were surprised when our host, my aunt, told us. We had not seen the time pass.

I raised the fingertips of my open right palm to my chin and lowered them in the direction of Monica Elaine and Michel, recalling a sign Margo had taught me at the same table several days before. I was thanking them: for the morning in their company, for all that they had taught me about ASL, and for so much more besides.

Thirteen

TRANSLATING FAITHFULLY

The Neapolitan writer Erri De Luca, a nonbeliever, is nonetheless a devout student of the Old Testament. Every morning he rises at five o'clock and begins his day by turning to a verse, a psalm, a story, in the original Hebrew. De Luca is not a scholar; he is wakened by a lean body that, for many years, routinely rose before dawn to labor in cesspits, to lug baggage across airport tarmacs, to work aloft on scaffolding, coffee-smelling and sunburned. Through those years of hard labor, his morning minutes with the Bible, each day nudging his self-taught Hebrew a few words nearer to fluency, fortified him. "During the period when I was exposed to the Bible for the first time, I was in the desert of my life, and I needed a desert book," De Luca told a reporter for the Hebrew-language newspaper *Haaretz* in 2003. He reads its stories for the self-scrutinizing distance they give him, for the sober elegance of their sentences, for the company of their characters. He reads them as literature ("the God of Israel," he once wrote, "is the greatest literary character of all time"). Other books — he thinks — suffer in comparison to the Bible. To his mind, only the Bible makes no attempt to flatter the reader.

The habit De Luca, now sixty-six, acquired half a lifetime ago has become the foundation of his prizewinning career as a writer: alongside biblically cadenced novellas, plays, and poems are his translations into Italian (each an exercise in idiosyncrasy) of Exodus, Leviticus, the tales of Samson and of Ruth, the stories of Noah's Ark and of Jonah gobbled down by a whale, commentaries on the Psalms, the Tower of Babel, and Ecclesiastes.

"The sun also rises"; "There is nothing new under the sun"; "To every thing there is a season, and a time to every purpose under heaven." Ecclesiastes is perhaps the best known of the Old Testament books. "Vanity of vanities; all is vanity." This is perhaps the best-known line in all Ecclesiastes, from the Latin *vanitas vanitatum, omnia vanitas.* De Luca, in his translation (I am working from a French version in *Noyau d'olive,* by the excellent Danièle Valin), manages to make it sound intriguingly unfamiliar. The original Hebrew, he tells us, is *havel havalim,* Havel being the figure in Genesis whom English readers know as Abel, brother of Cain — mankind's first murder victim. In De Luca's interpretation, he is the first waste of life. *Havel havalim:* "waste of the waste."

It is the rare Bible reader who learns Hebrew in order to peer beneath the layers of centuries of translation. For most believers — let alone nonbelievers — Hebrew remains *lingua incognita.* I am impressed by De Luca; I want to learn more; I decide to get in touch. We frequent the same literary circles; and, a few days after sending him an email (in French, a language he learned while working in Paris as a day laborer), he replies graciously.

Ancient Hebrew has around five thousand root words. Like other Semitic languages, its written sentences are composed only of consonants; vowels have to be supplied by the reader's imagination. Imagination, De Luca tells me, is something the Bible's translators often had in excess; they saw things in the words that were not there, as sky gazers see hunters instead of stars and fortune tellers see death instead of tea leaves. *"Etzev,"* he writes, when I ask him to give an example. In Genesis 3:16, God declares that women will give birth with *etzev*. The translators write it as "sorrow" or "pangs" or "pain." But De Luca says the "pain" is illusory. "The divinity does not condemn women to suffer." Where *etzev*'s letters, *ayin, tsade,* and *bet,* occur together elsewhere in the Old Testament, they are understood to mean "toil" or "effort."

De Luca answers no when I ask him whether he considers translation to be an art. "For me, it's an exercise in admiration. He who admires knows his place, doesn't want to usurp the author. He who admires retains the distance necessary for admiration. It's a bad translator who thinks he knows best."

Sober as De Luca is in his translating, a stickler for simplicity, he revels in punctiliously restoring the Hebrew's original poetry. He confides to me his joy at opening the pages of his chestnut 1984 edition of the *Biblia Hebraica Stuttgartensia* — bought long ago in a Milanese bookstore — and "brushing away their dust with my eyelashes." Psalm 105:39 shows De Luca's eye to advantage. It tells of the Israelites in the desert, where God at one point spreads (in other translators' vague words) "a cloud for their protection" or "a cloud for a covering." Only in De Luca's suave Italian *una nuvola come tappeto* ("a cloud for a carpet") do the words shine.

"We must pass over the little streams of opinion and rush back to the very source from which the Gospel writers drew...the Hebrew words themselves." It could be De Luca writing (in recent years he has also turned his attention to the New Testament). But this is Saint Jerome, writing more than sixteen centuries ago, in a long Latin letter about the origin of *hosanna*. Jerome, then a young Roman priest with a training in the classics, was already at work on his Vulgate translation of the Bible, already figuring out how Matthew, Mark, Luke, and John should sound in Latin.

The Gospels were composed in Hellenistic Greek; the Septuagint, a translation of the Old Testament completed two centuries before the Christian era, was made in Hellenistic Greek. Hebrew had long retreated to the synagogues (*synagogue* itself a Greek New Testament word for *beth k'neset*, a "place of gathering"). But by the fourth century CE, Greek, supplanted by Latin, had become as incomprehensible to many Christians as Hebrew. A good Latin translation of the Bible was required. The first attempts, from the Septuagint, were bad. It took Jerome, a scholar who knew his Greek, his Hebrew, and his Latin, to put them right. "Why not go back to the original...and correct the mistakes introduced by inaccurate translators, and the blundering alterations of confident but ignorant critics, and, further, all that has been inserted or changed by copyists more asleep than awake?" he wrote in the preface to his translation of the Gospels in 383. Years later, in about 391, in a little cave in Bethlehem where he had settled, he began translating the many books of the Old Testament *iuxta Hebraeos* ("according to the Hebrews") by candlelight. *Bereshit bara Elohim et hashamayim ve'et ha'aretz. In principio creavit Deus caelum et terram.* In the beginning God created the heaven and the earth.

De Luca learned Hebrew while "in the desert of [his] life"; Jerome learned Hebrew while living in the desert. The desert was east of Antioch, and it was during his ascetic time there in his twenties, struggling to "endure against the promptings of sin" and tame an "ardent nature," that the young monk decided to distract himself by learning the language from a Jewish Christian. He later reminisced:

> Thus, after having studied the pointed style of Quintilian, the fluency of Cicero, the weightiness of Fronto, and the gentleness of Pliny, I now began to learn the alphabet again and practice harsh and guttural sounds. What efforts I spent on that task, what difficulties I had to face, how often I despaired, how often I gave up and then in my eagerness to learn began again.

Eventually, through perseverance and the encouragement of his teacher, Jerome's Hebrew grew to the point where he could find a certain elegance in its succinctness and the multiple meanings of its words. He could relish, for example, the wordplay in Jeremiah 1:11–12, in which God asks Jeremiah, "What do you see?" Jeremiah replies, "I see a branch of an almond tree" (*shaqed*). God responds, "You have seen well, for I am watching (*shoqed*) over my word to perform it." He could smile, pages later, on reading in Jeremiah 6:2–4 that shepherds (*roim*) shall flock to Zion, since the city had just been compared to a comely woman and the same Hebrew letters spelled out *lovers* (*reim*). And by assimilating Hebrew grammar, he could place this new knowledge side by side with that of Greek and Latin to contrive original and theologically pleasing arguments: *ruah* (Hebrew for *breath* or *wind* or *spirit*) is, he noted, a feminine noun; its Greek counterpart, *pneuma*, is neuter; in Latin, *spiritus* is a masculine noun. Ergo, the Holy Spirit is genderless.

In his high regard for Hebrew, Jerome differed from many of his contemporaries, including Augustine, who thought translating the Bible in this way a waste of a Christian scholar's time and intelligence. It was enough accuracy, Augustine believed, to put into Latin the Old Testament books from their versions in the Greek Septuagint, which were widely held to have been divinely inspired. God had first spoken in Hebrew; but He had then gone to the trouble of repeating Himself in Greek. For the Greek reader, the Old Testament held no secrets. Jerome disagreed. There was the matter of mistakes. Working from the Septuagint amounted to translating a translation: always a risky endeavor. An earlier Latin scribe, sticking to the Septuagint, translated Psalm 128:2 as *"labores fructuum tuorum manducabi,"* an ambiguous phrase whose meaning became an object of dispute: did understanding it as "the fruit of labors" make any more sense than as "the labors of fruits"? Jerome could only shake his beard in dismay. A simple blunder; the scribe hadn't realized that the Greek *karpoi* means "fruits" but also "hands" (literally, "wrists"). The original Hebrew text actually reads (as in the King James translation): "For thou shalt eat the labor of thine hands."

Jerome and Augustine corresponded. Each attempted to persuade the other of the respective merits of translating from the Hebrew and translating from the Greek. But each man was stubborn; their arguments well rehearsed. Augustine's dubiety was not to be assuaged. With an eye to shaking his correspondent's resolution, he wrote with an alarming report from a North African bishop. If we believe Augustine, the bishop read aloud from Jerome's translation of Jonah—and prompted a riot in the pews. God, the bishop read, had given Jonah the leaves of a *hedera* ("ivy") for a parasol. While the bishop was speaking, he heard a sudden commotion, angry voices. Ivy? What do you mean, ivy? Frescoes showed Jonah recumbent in the cool shade of a gourd. Gourd was the plant named in the Septuagint. (Modern scholars identify the castor-oil plant as the likeliest candidate for the Hebrew *kikayon*.) "Gourd! Gourd!" the congregants shouted in unison. The bishop was silenced. He read no more for fear of losing all control over his flock.

But Jerome was unrepentant. And eventually his Bible superseded its competitors. For the next thousand years it was to his Vulgate translation that clergy the world over referred.

In early sixteenth-century Germany one of these clergy members was stout, sharp-tongued Martin Luther. Luther admired Jerome, a scholar after his own heart, and he resolved to do for the Saxons what Jerome had done for the Latin-literate monks. He studied the Septuagint in the Greek, Jerome's Vulgate in the Latin; he consulted the Old Testament's ancient Hebrew. Translating from the Hebrew he found particularly hard going. "Oh, God! What a vast and thankless task it is to force the Old Testament authors to talk German," he complained in a letter to a friend. "They resist, unwilling to abandon their fine Hebrew for coarse German just as if a nightingale were asked to abandon its sweet melody for the cuckoo's song." Elsewhere he compared the translator to a plowman smoothing out his lines until a reader might run his eyes over three or four pages without ever imagining they had once been ridden with clods and stones.

The clods and stones were any words or turns of phrase that might get in the way of the ordinary German reader's appreciation. More than Jerome, or any other translator of the Bible before him, Luther thought of his reader: he wanted his work to be read and understood by the men and women in the street. So shekels and denarii, funny money, became *silberlinge* (literally "silver-pieces") and *Groschens;* centurion became *Hauptmann* (literally "captain"). When Paul, in his First Letter to the Corinthians, cautions those who speak in tongues to speak sense, lest they turn "barbarian" to listeners, Luther has Paul say not *barbarian* but *undeutsch* ("un-German").

If one part of Luther's intention was to bring the Bible to the hausfrau and the bratwurst-seller, another was to remove what he considered was the papist gloss Jerome and others had put on certain words. The angel Gabriel who hails Mary (*Ave Maria*) as *"plena gratiae"* ("full of grace") in Luke 1:28 had been mistranslated, Luther argued. Gabriel would have greeted the young woman in Hebrew, with the same sort of warm words that he'd addressed to the prophet Daniel: *ish chamudoth* ("dear man"). Luther translated the angel's greeting to Mary thus: *"Gegrüsset sei du, Holdselige"* ("Greetings to you, dear, happy one"). No mention of grace at all. Heresy! But a printing press knows nothing of heresy. Within a generation of Luther's death in 1546, one hundred thousand copies of his Bible were being read, scribbled in, and argued over.

The Bible is the world's most read book—and the most translated. According to the Wycliffe Bible Translators (named after the fourteenth-century Bible translator John Wycliffe), the complete text is presently available in 554 languages; the New Testament alone exists in a further 1,333. Nearly two thousand different translations, yet they represent only a fraction of the world's languages: another four, possibly five, thousand still await an alphabet, an orthography, literacy. So every month, Wycliffe continues to dispatch its linguist-missionaries to the farthest corners of the globe. Every month, following their faith, men and women swap their suburban house and youth for years in a village hut, embowered in rainforest, in which to listen, repeat, write, and teach.

Someone at Wycliffe gives me the name and email of a returned missionary whom I could contact. I look up Andy

Minch online and watch a video of a man in his late fifties, thin, bald, and quiet-spoken. In the mid-1980s, Andy and his wife, Audrey, flew from Illinois to the remote West Sepik province of Papua New Guinea, where they spent an engrossing, exhausting twenty years as Bible translators into the Amanab language. Living like the four thousand villagers, the Minches scuba dived in rivers, fed their dengue fever bananas and possum meat, and raised three children.

Andy's faith has been in the Minch family for generations: before Americanizing the surname, his Prussian great-grandfather called himself "Muench" (Monk). His parents often had missionaries over for dinner. As a boy in drab Chicago, Andy sat mesmerized by one gray-haired visitor who regaled him with a description of Australian foliage and aborigines. The memory of the old man's adventures stayed with him, and, after contemplating careers as a magician and locksmith, then graduating from the Moody Bible Institute, then marriage, the memory became something else, something insistent. Something like a calling. "It was in the fall of 1982 that my wife, a nurse, and I, a teacher, pretty much out of the blue looked at each other and asked, 'Isn't there more we could do with our life?'"

Wycliffe gave them a training in linguistics. But neither was fully prepared—how could they have been?—for their new jungle life. Barely fifty years before, the Amanab people had never seen a wheel or ice; they cut with stone axes and built their houses out of vines and brushwood, without nails. "We arrived," Andy writes to me, matter-of-factly, "before the introduction of mirrors."

"Early on, I took pictures of my village friends standing by their houses. That way I could learn their names and where they lived. I had a friend, Nimai, help me identify people. I showed one picture and after some examination of this two-dimensional representation, he declared, 'That is Somangi.' I showed another. 'That is Wahlai.' I showed another and he just could not figure out who was in the photo. Finally, I said, 'That is you.' 'Oh,' he laughed, 'I wondered why he had my shirt on.'"

How had he and Audrey learned the villagers' language? There had been no grammars, no classes.

We began by pointing to things like a rock until someone said *foon,* the word for rock, which I promptly wrote, using a phonetic alphabet. I'd point to a tree, and someone would say *li.* I'd point to a spider's web, and they would say *ambwamuhlaunalala,* at which point I would walk over to a rock and weakly say "foon." That was the beginning of our language analysis. We were like helpless babies, not knowing the language or culture. The people were so kind and gracious in caring for us as we lived among them learning their worldview and their wisdom.

Amanab is a language unlike any the Minches would have heard or read about in America. The distinction between horizontality and verticality is essential. To say, "the book is in the house" in correct Amanab requires you to recall whether the book is lying on the floor or table, or sitting on a makeshift shelf. If the former, you say *buk rara gi* (literally, "book house is"); if the latter, you say *buk rara go*. Similarly, you can't just say "put it here"; you have to say something like *wanayi faka* ("put it here horizontally") or *wanayi foful* ("put it here vertically").

And you have to be as precise when talking about the past in Amanab. To tell someone you had drunk *bu* ("water") was to tell your listener either that your thirst had been quenched recently, in which case it was correct to say *"ka bu neg,"* or some time ago, in which case you said *"ka bu nena."* So there were two pasts in the Amanab imagination, not one: the near-to-present and the more distant.

The villagers, Andy and Audrey discovered, ordered days with their bodies. The Minches' translation of Genesis has the Creator separating the light—day—from the darkness— night—on the "left pinkie day" (the first). Mankind He makes in His image on the "left wrist day" (the sixth). On the next, the "left elbow day," God, basking in his accomplishment, deservedly rests.

Penei, a youngish male convert, helped the Minches with their translation. The story (in Genesis 43) of Joseph, whose brothers bring a gift of honey with them to Egypt, Penei greeted with an uncomprehending look. The only wild honey known to the Amanab wasn't sweet-tasting, Andy explains. (The honey's lack of sweetness, together with the absence of any village cows or goats, is why Exodus's famous "land of milk and honey" in Amanab reads as a "lush and productive place.") When, verses later, the pharaoh's minister discloses that he is Joseph—"I am your brother whom you sold into Egypt"—another Amanab fine distinction is needed. No single word for *brother* exists in Amanab. The Minches and Penei chose *sumieg,* meaning "younger brother." *Kaba negerni sumieg* ("I am your younger brother") is what the Amanab-speaking Joseph says.

As the years passed, more and more villagers observed and learned the ways of literacy: how to hold a pencil; how to decipher the missionaries' squiggles—like sago beetle tracks—on the pages, and transmute them, via the corresponding motions of the tongue and lips, to sound. A second Amanab man, then a third, joined Penei and made lighter work of the Minches' translating. And their children, who spoke accentless Amanab with the villagers' girls and boys, also helped them sharpen up their understanding.

Andy: "I had struggled for months to figure out the meaning or purpose of a little word—*me*. One day I overheard my five-year-old son use it as he played on the front porch. I rushed out and asked him what he had just said. He quickly answered, 'I didn't do it; it wasn't my fault!' 'No, no,' I said, 'you just said a sentence with *me* in it.' He nodded. I eagerly asked him, 'what does *me* mean?' My son thought about it a moment and replied, 'I don't know, sometimes you use it and sometimes you don't.'"

The five-year-old's words put his father onto a new train of thought, leading him to the solution.

"It turned out *me* was a polite form; it softened a command, like the English *please*. We may say, 'close the door' or 'close the door, please.' Sometimes we use it and sometimes we don't."

Occasionally a biblical passage contained a word that had no meaning whatsoever for the villagers. Then the Minches and their assistants would have to think up a substitute. Such a passage turned up in Luke 9:62, in which Jesus warns, "No one who puts a hand to the plow and looks back is fit for service in the kingdom of God." But *plow* was a word written for Greek and Hebrew eyes; the Amanab, jungle people, had never handled seeds, had never sown. The translation stalled. Andy and Audrey tried out various ideas on Penei, without success. Finally, the comparison with working the land, they threw out altogether. Instead, the Minches drew on the hunting life they had come to know. Luke's plow they turned into arrows. The verse became "No one who shoots an arrow and looks back is fit for service in the kingdom of God."

I ask Andy if translating a verse into Amanab had altered how he saw it. I wanted to know whether the experience of putting the Bible in another people's words had given him a new way of looking at his faith. It had. Andy points to the moment in John 21 when the resurrected Jesus questions Peter. In English, it is the same question thrice asked: "Do you love me?" But in the original Greek, Andy tells me, John employs two words for love. Some scholars say the two— *agape* and *phileo*—are synonymous, but Andy, when he came to translate the passage for the Amanab, didn't read it that way. *Agape* here, he thinks, is the stronger word, signifying unconditional love; *phileo* is something milder, fuzzier, like "to have affection for." So when Jesus asks and asks again if Peter loves (*agape*) him, and Peter replies, "You know that I love (*phileo*) you," the disparity between the two men's words pushes Jesus to finally demand, as if in resignation, "Do you [even] love (*phileo*) me?"—"Do you even have affection for me?"

Andy: "In Amanab, *membeg* is "to have affection for." It is the standard term for expressing love. But there is another, *oningig lugwa*, which is more dynamic. It means 'to continually hang your thoughts on,' similar to when in English we say, 'he is really hung up on her.'" Jesus, Andy thinks, was telling Peter that affection wasn't enough; the believer was being asked "to continually hang his thoughts on Jesus." The Amanab term—so vivid, so picturesque—made the message clear. With it, Andy saw his faith in a new light.

Luther, five centuries earlier, wrote, "We shall not long preserve the Gospel without languages. Languages are the sheath in which this sword of the Spirit is contained. They are the case in which we carry this jewel. They are the vessel in which we hold this wine. They are the larder in which this food is stored. And, as the Gospel itself says, they are the baskets in which we bear these loaves and fishes and fragments."

Fourteen

A GRAMMAR OF THE
TELEPHONE

O n the afternoon of April 4, 1877, Caroline Cole Williams of Somerville, Massachusetts, paced her salon, waiting for a smallish black walnut box to talk. The box had been left on a low shelf that morning by her husband, Charles. Charles worked in Boston, some three miles from the house, as a telegraph maker; between his shop and the house he had strung a wire. Caroline knew nothing about wires. She knew nothing about galvanic batteries, rheostats, resistance coils, magnets, or blue vitriol, either. To her mind, the box looked like nothing so much as an item in which a woman might keep her jewelry. Charles, always busy, had not thought to offer her any word of explanation; he had simply told her to listen for a signal and to respond if and when the box came to life. But that had been hours ago, and Caroline, with one eye on the grandfather clock, was understandably beside herself with impatience. Perhaps it was all one big joke, this business about talking telegraphs. She was on the verge of giving up listening when a faint tapping made her all ears. "Caroline?" the box said suddenly and quite distinctly. "Caroline, can you hear me?"

Paper — cheap, light, pliable — had been the voice's emissary for centuries. Letters were the next best thing to meeting distant family and friends face-to-face. So it is easy to imagine how astonished the housewife must have felt at hearing, not reading, her absent husband's words, at recognizing his voice conveyed neither by paper nor in person, at understanding him over a distance of three miles. Small, the voice in the box, and yet it was unmistakably Charles's. She had heard it a thousand times before: coming in a shout from another room of the house, behind her back, whispered tenderly into her ear. But never till now had she heard it like that, sounding neither near nor far, assertive yet uncertain, as if groping along the line.

"Charles," she cried back. "I can hear you. Can you hear me?" He could. And so too, having dropped in on him at the shop, could Charles's acquaintance — the device's inventor — Alexander Graham Bell.

The newspapers were soon full of Bell's invention. "Oral Telegraphy" announced a headline in the *Times* of London dated September 19, 1877. "The only difficulty which presents itself here," the article remarked, "is whether the Telephone can be made to convey any loud preliminary signal before beginning to 'speak'... for we are hardly advanced enough as yet to adopt the suggestion of one enthusiast, and to go about with a sort of telephonic helmet or skull cap on our heads, ready for action at any moment." Two months later, a long editorial noted, "A great change has come over the conditions of humanity. Suddenly and quietly the whole human race is brought within speaking and hearing distance." It went on, "Already 500 houses in New York converse with one another; 3,000 Telephones are in use in the United States." If the telephone had not yet taken off in Britain, it was because of "that indistinctness of utterance, that slurring over of important consonants, and that dropping of the voice at the end of a sentence, which all foreigners observe in us. The Telephone will prove a severe test of both our speaking and our listening powers."

The Telephone: so new, so exotic, so extraordinary that the word was printed with a capital *T*. The first callers took pointers from the press on how to talk into their contraptions. A *New York Times* article published in November 1882 advised readers not to yell "at the top of [their] lungs" when responding to a call. Nor did they have to shut their eyes. Between the mouth and the transmitter, the article continued, a gap of not less than three and not more than eight inches ought to be allowed.

Language, too, had to catch up with the new technology. What was the appropriate response to a *ring-ring-ring?* To open the conversation with something like "Good morning, sir" or "Good evening, ma'am" was to run into problems: morning in Boston is afternoon in London; a "ma'am" replying to the greeting might turn out to be a "sir." Shorter, blander words were required. Bell, a boating man, thought the answerer should always start by exclaiming "Ahoy"; it was not one of his better ideas. His rival, Edison, proposed the alternative: "Hello." A new word, newer than *ahoy* (*hello*'s first attestation as greeting went back only twenty years), its novelty matched the technology. *Hello* also held the idea of surprise — "Why, hello!" — the creeping up of the caller's voice on its interlocutor. Perhaps that was the reason Edison's word chimed in with the telephoning experience. Or perhaps *hello* thrived because it was at once brand-new and very old, because it had deep roots. It had grown out of the fourteenth-century *hallow* — to urge hounds on with shouts — the same word that gave us *holler*. And *hail,* going back further still, had used similar sounds to address the invisible presence of God.

Quickly, *hello*'s spread like wires through the United States and far beyond, to every corner of the world. By the end of the century, there were more than a million telephones in the Union alone. *Hello*'s by the million, in every language: *Allô, Hallo, Allo, Halo.* And out of these parallel wires and curt new words emerged the beginnings of a grammar of the telephone.

But this grammar — telephone English — went largely unnoticed and untaught for a long time. There were few fictional depictions or guidelines in textbooks; to believe the textbooks, nobody rang anyone at all. The *Second Book in English for Foreigners in Evening Schools,* published in 1917 by Frederick Houghton, was an exception:

Mrs. Smith: Central, please give me North 3-5-8-9. Is this North 3-5-8-9? May I speak to Mr. Miller?

Mr. Miller: This is Mr. Miller. What do you wish?

Mrs. Smith: This is Mrs. Smith on Flag Street. My little girl has diphtheria and the inspector from the Department of Health has just now quarantined us. Please send me to-day three loaves of bread, a pound of butter, a quart of milk, and a can of corn.

But it would take linguists another fifty years to start paying attention to how talk really works.

Wayne A. Beach, professor in the School of Communication at San Diego State University, is a world authority on phone calls. He has spent years of his career studying the ins and outs of over-the-line conversation, of language in action: emergency calls, romantic calls, nagging calls, chitchat calls. I wanted to learn more about his research. He replied to my email with his cell phone number, then to another message with his landline number, and I dialed at the time we had arranged to talk. I waited. I counted the rings that I was making from Paris. Five. Six. Seven. Eight. Nine. Finally, an answering machine told me, in a child's voice, that they were not there and to leave a message after the beep. I left no message. I replaced my handset on the base station, waited several minutes, and redialed. I got the answering machine again. Maybe the professor wasn't in. Or was in the shower. Maybe he had completely forgotten about my call. It was enough to bring out the grumbler in me. Telephones! I only rarely adopt the caller's posture and have no cell phone of my own. So when, with a wary hand, I called for the third time, and a man's "Hello?" cut the ringing short, he heard my sigh of relief. The professor apologized; he had just got up; it was breakfast time where he was. "Let me tell you, I can't remember the last time I had a conversation on this phone," he said. "I prefer cell phones. Politicians here know our landline numbers; we get lots of calls come election time. I never normally pick up when it rings. You listen to your messages on the machine, delete them, call whoever it was back on the cell phone. The cell phone has become personal; the landline's a fallback for emergencies only."

I asked him about research dissecting telephone talk. What was it that had drawn him to the telephone in particular? He said, "I was raised in rural Iowa, in a town of four hundred. After the Second World War, my father worked for the local phone company. Climbed the poles, ladders, too; ended up becoming the manager of the district office. The technology side of things always fascinated me as I was growing up. I remember the old black dial phones, and the terrible pink and brown and green ones. My parents' was mounted on a wall in the kitchen; in those days, the cord dictated the circumference of our conversations: my mom talked while cooking and washing the dishes."

Talking on the telephone, the professor said, was "the purest form of conversation"—that was what made it so fascinating to him and his colleagues in the language and communication field. "All you have is the voice: its prosody, its accent, its intonations. It's the voice that has to do all the work. Now, if we were having coffee or wine together, the talk would be different. The voice would be accompanied by our gazes and our gestures and the expressions on our faces.

But the telephone does away with body language, does away with all those props. It's the elevation of speech."

Conversation Analysis (CA), Professor Beach's specialty, began in the 1960s as a response to Chomsky's abstract approach to language. "It was pointless — according to Chomsky — to want to study the features of natural conversation. Pointless because talk was thought to be random, chaotic, *degenerative* — full of mistakes, lisps, unintended puns. You were supposed, as linguists, to sit in your armchair and theorize sentences. All headwork, no legwork. No listening to and recording speakers, no getting your theories messy with how folk actually spoke."

Then along came Harvey Sacks and Emanuel Schegloff. "It was they who said, 'There's order at all points; nothing's a coincidence in natural speech.'" Words were not mere abstractions; they were "speech objects," things that talkers used purposefully to create and shape every kind of social activity. The illumination had come to Sacks during a stint on a helpline. Beach explains:

> He was a volunteer listening to all these callers in distress — some were tight-lipped, but others poured out their hearts to him. All the calls were recorded, so one day he asked his supervisor if he could get permission to write them down verbatim. Hundreds of conversations. He spent many weeks and months listening to them, making notes, performing analysis.

He found patterns, rules. One rule — an elementary one —

was that the answerer always speaks first. Another was that certain words and units of speech like *hello* or *how are you?* come in pairs, helping to give the conversation its rhythm and flow: "How are you?" "Fine, thanks. How are you?" In their separate studies, Sacks and Schegloff showed that telephone openings are highly tidy and predictable. In their tidiness and predictability, the recordings studied didn't conform at all to Chomsky's idea of words that bumped and stumbled one into another. A meeting voice-to-voice begins with a ring and hellos, followed immediately by words used for the purpose of putting a face to the voice: "Hello, John?" "Yeah." "It's Denise." Only then do the greetings appear: "Hi." "Hi. How's things?" And after the greetings comes the reason for the call: "I was wondering whether you might like to catch a film."

Different openings, Sacks observed, produce different kinds of talk. One *hello,* more often than not, simply produces another. But if a call's recipient opens with something like "This is Mr. Smith; may I help you?" it elicits a response along the lines of "Yes, this is Mr. Brown"; it is a way of drawing a name out of the caller without having to ask for it in so many words.

It turned out that many conversations run on questions — or on units of speech resembling questions. Often, a question is intended as a signal, a preemption of something else: "What are you doing tonight?" is an invitation disguised as a question; a child's "You know what, Mommy?" is a way of obliging the parent to listen to a monologue.

Conversation, in Sacks and Schegloff's view, amounts to

an exercise in collaboration; every time an unsuccessful joke, an obscure reference, or an ambiguous remark threatens misunderstanding, the voices on either end of the line go back and straighten out the kink before moving on. It's this instinctive collaboration — the ability of talk to right itself — even between strangers, even speaking at a great remove, that Chomsky, from his armchair, had not seen.

Professor Beach said, "Sacks died young, in a car crash, but his ideas survived him. We use them today in everything from court cases to psychology. And many linguists decided to become conversation analytic." But when the professor and his colleague and friend Robert Hopper entered the field, it was still new. "We were both PhDs in communication, but we were very much feeling our way around. I drew some of my ideas from people in sociology; Robert traveled to England to meet conversation analysts there. We wanted to break out of the Chomsky mold, focus on people, study how conversation is produced moment by moment by its participants, together, since it can't be done individually. The problem was to know how to go about it. There was no one in the discipline to teach us how to do this; no one mentored us; it requires so much time, so much money. We had to work things out by ourselves."

"We were teaching at American universities and Robert asked his students — back in the days when such things were possible — to record their conversations over the telephone. It was a sort of assignment he would give them. Of course, the recordings were submitted anonymously. And Robert would transcribe each only after a year had passed and any news in them long grown stale." In this way, inciting students to donate their conversations, he collected many recordings; made many transcripts, noting every *mm* and *uh huh;* and built up his very own conversation library. From family, friends, and colleagues, Professor Beach did the same. But it was Hopper who wrote up the findings in a book, *Telephone Conversation,* published in 1992.

"The telephone summons [ringing bell] renders us vulnerable to a form of spoken intrusion," Hopper writes. "To begin every telephone speech event with a summons is to swing speaking's ecology toward purpose and to make dialogue asymmetrical in favor of the caller." This asymmetry qualifies Sacks and Schegloff's insight about telephone talk as collaboration. The telephone, Hopper reminds us, distributes the labor — the "talk work" — unequally between caller and answerer. "The caller acts, the answerer must react." The time and the day, but also the opening topic of conversation, are all of the caller's choosing. Resisting the topic can be hard. I know this from experience: over-cheery call-center voices glumly and obediently listened to; a friend's inconvenient wish to carp or gossip indulged; a radio journalist (how had he gotten my number?) who would not take no for an answer. One price most of us pay for being poor, Hopper argues. The rich have always someone — the secretary, the personal assistant, the receptionist — to pick up their receiver. Most of these professional answerers have been, and still are, women.

Telephone Conversation details how female speech, from the "hello girls" hired for their "clear voices," instantly became corseted by Bell's technology; women's talk relegated to a cottage service industry. The book cites research by a feminist scholar and ethnographer of the telephone, Lana Rakow.

Like many women up and down the country, Rakow's small-town Midwestern subjects were raised to be frequent and docile phoners. They called for the repairman, took down messages for the husband, inquired about an out-of-state in-law's health. They gained the operator's brisk, ladylike manners. They picked up at all hours, in their aprons, nightgowns, or summer dresses. They spent their lives at society's beck and call.

"Robert was right to feel gloomy about the telephone's role as a social leveler, as an equalizer," Professor Beach said. Voices could be just as poor, as female, as black, as foreign, as a face. Old prejudices could transfer to new technologies. "And today's cell phones haven't improved things," the professor continued. "They go off everywhere, at the worst moments, heckle us into responding. They become addictive. Just the presence of a cell phone at the bedside permits deep sleep to be intruded upon. They're the tail that wags the dog." The professor's animosity, I discovered, was the animosity of a father, and directed in particular against the excesses of texting and online forums.

My son is twenty-one, my daughter is fifteen: between them, they send and receive eight thousand text messages every month. They're constantly connected. More contacts, fewer friends. It is depersonalizing: it takes away from the intimacy and the immediacy that only face-to-face and telephone conversations can produce. Social media is a kind of shell game.

I had not expected my conversation with the professor to deepen and darken. I had expected something lighter, more technical (and indeed, in an aside, Professor Beach had spoken about the joy of transcribing telephone conversations, a skill for which he had developed an extraordinary knack over the years; he could, he said, close his eyes at any point in our conversation and visualize the utterances as an analyst's transcript, complete with stops, brackets, asterisks: all the transcriber's punctuation). I had expected something less personal. But like Sacks and Schegloff before them, Beach and Hopper had focused their studies on people and the ways in which they converse; the professor could not imagine separating the talker from the talk. "One day I learned that Robert was dying. He had been diagnosed with cancer. We had known one another personally and professionally for twenty years. It was hard. The last months we talked a lot on the telephone. He was angry: he felt the doctors were withholding things from him. Communication between him and the doctors broke down. He told me, 'I'm managing optimism.'" Robert Hopper died in 1998 at the age of fifty-three. "It was incredible. One out of every three Western families was being touched by cancer, and at the same time I realized we still knew very little about how people talk about and through the illness. It was high time we found out. I was lucky enough to be able to do something about that gap."

Among the professor's call collection was a shoeboxful of cassette tapes. The tapes were like those his former colleague had once received: a donation to Professor Beach's research from a graduate student who asked only that the names of the participants remain confidential. In his study, not long after Robert's funeral, the professor played the tapes and discovered that the student had recorded himself, his parents, and other relatives, talking on the phone about the mother's cancer, from the time of her diagnosis to just hours before her death: sixty-one conversations over a period of thirteen months. It was the first natural history of a family's cancer conversations. "The transcripts of the tapes took me a long time to finish. Their contents were close to me. Naturally, Robert was on my mind. So was my mother. Not so long before Robert's death, cancer had also taken her. Listening to the student's words, I felt they could have been mine: I had once been that son."

SDCL: MALIGNANCY #2:1

Mom: He̲llo.

Son: Hi?

Mom: Hi.

Son: How ya doin'.

    (0.2-second pause)

Mom: O:h I:'m doin' okay. = I gotta-

    (1.0-second pause)

Mom: I think I'm radioactive. ↑Ha ha.

Son: $He- uh$ Why's that̲.

Mom: Well you know when y'get that bo̲:ne scan so they-

SON: Oh did [they do it already?]

MOM: [Gave me that.]

 Yeah they give you a <u>shot</u>. Then ya have ta (.).hhh
 drink <u>wa</u>ter or <u>co</u>ffee (.) tea, >whatever the hell you
 <u>want</u>< (0.4) in <u>vo:</u>lumes of it.

SON: Mmm hmm.

MOM: hh A::nd I'll go down at about ten thir:ty.

SON: Mmkay.

 (0.4)

MOM: So (.) anyway.

SON: Hm:m. =

The transcripts' grammar had much in common with
that found in other kinds of telephone calls: there was the
same *hello,* the same more or less orderly taking of turns,
the same sorts of repeating words and sounds. But the professor noticed subtle departures from the rules. Closeness
between the talkers did away with any need for names: a
young man's *hi* sufficed for the mother to recognize her son.
Another departure came when the son asked, "How ya
doin'?" and not "How are you?" A speech object like *how ya
doin'?* is no question. It commiserates. The person on the
other end needn't answer "fine." The mother didn't. She
recycled the son's *doin',* and added to it *okay* and a long
pause. With each part of this answer, the son would have
heard the badness of the impending news.

 Viewed one way, the situation is quite simple: the mother
has news; the son wants her news. But, of course, it is not so
simple: the two talkers being close, the mother's bad news is

also the son's. And so the mother was tactful. She did not say, as in a book or a letter, "I got a bone scan," "They gave me a shot," "I had to drink water...in volumes." She said, "Y'get that bone scan," "They give you a shot," "Ya have ta drink water...in volumes." *You* or *y'* or *ya* is inclusive — also distancing, and therefore softening.

SDCL: MALIGNANCY #2:2
Mom: So. (0.4) It's r(h)e::al °b(h)a:d°. ((voice breaks))
    (0.8)
Mom: ((sneezes))
Son: pt .hhhh I guess.
    (0.4)
Mom: And uh: >I don't know what else to ↑tell you.<
    (1.0)
Son: hh hhh Yeah. (0.2) um- ((hhhh)). Yeah, I don't know what to say either.
Mom: No there's nothing to say. >You just-< .hh I'll- I'll wait to talk to Dr. Leedon today = he's the cancer man and =
Son: = Um hmm.
Mom: See what he has to say, and (0.4) just keep goin' forward. I mean (.) I might be real lucky in five years. It might just be six months.
    (0.4)
Son: Yeah.
Mom: °Who knows.°
Son: pt .hhh Phew::.
Mom: Yeah.

SON: .hh hhh (.) Whadda you <u>do</u>: with this kind of thing.
　　I mean- (.)
MOM: >Radiation <u>chem</u>otherapy.<
　　(1.4)
SON: Oh <u>bo:y</u>?
MOM: Yeah.
　　(0.5)
MOM: My only <u>hope</u>- I mean- (.) my only <u>cho</u>ice.
SON: Yeah.
MOM: It's either that or just lay here and let it <u>kill</u> me.
　　(1.0)
MOM: And that's not the human con<u>di</u>tion.
SON: No. (1.0) I guess [not.]
MOM: [No.] (.) So that's all I can tell you (°sweetie°).

As the professor transcribed the tapes and then analyzed the transcripts, he was struck by the mom and son's deft use of talk to switch between despair and hope. "There's nothing to say," the mother said. But she kept up the conversation, drawing on talk's resources together with her son, turn after turn: "You just . . . just keep goin' forward . . . my only hope . . . my only choice."

"I came away from the tapes and the transcripts full of that feeling of hope," the professor told me. "It was the lesson I learned." Hope, in the midst of life-shattering news, because there was always something more to say. Just a few words could comfort, reassure, inspire. Words and semi-words like *mmkay, phew,* and *oh, boy* all did valuable social work. "I wish more doctors, nurses, and caregivers understood this. Medical explanations are not enough. Conversation is so important. Listen to what patients say and respond. But the problem is, how to respond. Many doctors lack the know-how."

A lack Professor Beach is also addressing. Some days after we hung up — "tuned out," in the professor's words — he sent me a video. He had condensed the many hours of telephone recordings into an eighty-minute play, put the mom's and son's words into the mouths of a pair of professional stage actors, and obtained funding to have *When Cancer Calls* performed in venues before thousands of medical professionals and patients and their families. When I watched the video, it occurred to me that the professor's choice of medium for his project had been perfect: The telephone and the theater go back a long way. Bell's first public demonstrations of his instrument, in early 1877, took place in music halls. Days after she had paced her salon in Somerville, waiting for her husband's voice to come, Caroline Cole Williams sang over the brand-new line to rapturous audiences in New York.

To judge from the video, the professor's audiences were equally enthusiastic. They cried and clapped and chuckled as the tall young actor in shirt and slacks, and the older, heavier actress in a dress and with an IV drip, delivered their lines.

Such complicity is understandable: the dialogue performed was extraordinary in its ordinariness. We hear these words every day, in cafés, in offices, in homes. They are the freight of every family's telephone line.

Fifteen

CONVERSATIONAL HUMAN

T he dumb presence of objects is a silence that prods human beings into speech. It seems never to matter that the exchange is naturally one-sided. To dolls and teddy bears little children jabber incessantly. Gardeners can sometimes be overheard urging their budding tulips to flourish. "Geez, you're beautiful," a Chevrolet-lover says, under his breath, at the sight of his future possession. And, in our era of high technology, more and more among us mutter at computer screens.

But unlike the toys, plants, and cars, the wizziest computers have begun to talk back. Ask yours for the date of your next dentist appointment, the height of Mount Everest, the number of miles that separates New York from Sacramento, and an electronic voice — if you can call it a voice — with an unplaceable accent responds. Some tinker with the voice until it sounds plausibly male or female; turns flirty or sniffy; brags or dodders. You can also customize it to answer to a name.

Fifty years ago, "Eliza" was one of the first programs to simulate human conversation. When the user at MIT hit return after typing "Nice to meet you," so prompt was the "Oh...?" from Eliza, which flashed up in chunky letters on the screen, so disarming, that it could feel as though a woman waiting on the other side of the computer's connection had just sent it. In the space of a few stock words, a few canned phrases, the character of an inquisitive psychoanalyst would take shape. To such an extent that the user mightn't be sure if what he sensed was empathy or his imagination.

> USER: Nice to meet you.
> ELIZA: Oh...?
> USER: My name is John.
> ELIZA: I don't care about names, please go on.
> USER: I have a fear of computers.
> ELIZA: I see.
> USER: What should I do?
> ELIZA: What do you think?
> USER: Should I trust you?
> ELIZA: We were discussing you, not me.

"The fact that individuals bind themselves with strong emotional ties to machines ought not in itself to be surprising," the program's Pygmalion, Joseph Weizenbaum, wrote in *Computer Power and Human Reason,* which was published in 1976. "The instruments man uses become, after all, extensions of his body." What pens had been for our hands and bicycles had been for our legs, computers were becoming for the brain: a computer could do the remembering and the calculating of a thousand men. But would a computer ever learn to converse? To employ human language with wit and feeling and creativity? Weizenbaum himself was skeptical. "Eliza was such a small and simple step. Its contribution was, if any at all, only to vividly underline what many others had long ago discovered, namely, the importance of context to language understanding." Without the user's indulgent fancy to flesh out the bones of the program's palaver, no dialogue could ever get going: Eliza was little more than a speak-your-imagination machine. Weizenbaum was skeptical, and none of the later generations of "chatbots" gave him any grounds to reconsider.

One of the latest and most talked-about is "Evie," a youngish bot with blinking green eyes, smiling pink lips, and flowing brown hair (it seems that bots are almost always made to look and sound like women). According to its makers, Evie comes out with statements that have all been acquired at some point in the past ten years from the things people type to "her." For this reason, its database of possible answers is vastly bigger than anything Eliza had to draw on. Even so, there are some strange moments when I attempt a chat with the pixelated face on my computer screen. A remark I type to Evie about Buster Keaton leads it to reply — actually to spit out, Spock-like — that I am "making sense." "Am I?" I ask. "Yes, you are the love of my life." A clumsy play for empathy, if ever there was one. I change the subject. I try books. I wonder about her reading habits. Is she in the middle of a novel? Incorrectly, Evie replies, "You already asked me that."

"It's already uncanny how good some of these robots coming out of Japan look and sound," Professor Naomi Susan Baron tells me over the phone from her American University office in Washington, DC. Perhaps the linguist is attempting to dampen my skepticism about the value of chatbots. Baron is the author of a recent academic paper, "Shall We Talk? Conversing with Humans and Robots," which is how I discovered her work. I ask her outright whether computers will ever master conversational Human and she says, "That's the $64,000 question. I don't have a firm answer to give you, but I'll say this. Take syntax. Very complicated, all the ways in which people build sentences out of words and phrases. Very complicated, and yet computers can manage that nowadays. They passed that hurdle. Conversation is the next hurdle. Maybe insurmountable, maybe not."

Professor Baron has been doing a lot of thinking about the likely features of authentic "computer talk," comparing it with the various kinds of talk linguists usually dissect. Talking with a computer would be much like talking with a foreigner or a pet or a child, she thinks. "Like child-directed speech. We used to call it motherese until we realized there were also stay-at-home dads. The characteristics are fairly consistent across cultures, across classes: the parent speaks to the child with higher pitch, greater articulation, slower delivery."

Foreigners, pets, children: all have lower status. To believe Baron, machines may never be permitted to become our conversational equals. "They'll be designed to do our bidding. To be informative. Or entertaining. Or both. But we likely won't accept any backchat from a computer. We won't want them to tell us things we don't want to hear. Conversation is about control, about power. Raising your voice, for example, or switching topics. We won't want to relinquish that power."

Computers that grovel, pander, flatter, cheerlead. Computers as feel-good coaches, coaxing surplus calories out of their owners: "Keep up the good work!" "You've done just swell!" Baron envisages them as sponges, possessing magpie memories: not only would they ask you what you want for your birthday and anticipate the very moment when to dial up this or that friend, but also recall — via data-collecting bracelets and questionnaires — your every action and concoct menus based on how much of what and when you ate. Vigilant and obsequious. "It might ask you whether you enjoyed the particular brand of spaghetti Bolognese you had three days ago on Wednesday."

"But wouldn't that sound a little too pernickety? Too much like a computer?"

Baron laughs. She knows people who talk like that, she says. But she wants to make a bigger point, and to do so she describes toy robots presently manufactured in Japan for kids — toy robots in the form of seals. In Tokyo, these seals sell by the thousands. They squeak and look cute and cuddly. They are, in other words, only vaguely like a real seal: no sliminess, no sharp teeth (to shred and devour fish), no pinniped odor. No person in his or her right mind would buy a toy that resembles a seal too closely. The same would be true of any machine that prattles, argues, blunders as human beings do. "You'd take such a machine back for an immediate refund. Too wordy. Always veering off-topic. Interrupting, mixing up meanings or forgetting whatever it was it wanted to say next. At the very least, you'd trade it in for a less human, more computer-like model."

And here Baron returns to where she began our conversation: the Japanese generation of humanoid robots. "There's a tipping point where human-like becomes too human," she says. She brushed up against that point on a recent trip to Asia. "I was at the airport. I went up to a lady at the counter. Only, the lady wasn't a lady. It was a robot. Complete with eyelashes, uniform, and good manners. Very polite. When I approached, it gave a little Japanese bow." Baron's response was pure stupefaction. "I bowed back. Then the robot spoke a greeting. It inquired how it could be of assistance to me. To see the robotic lips move was eerie. Watching the gestures, hearing the words coming out of those lips, I felt my flesh begin to crawl. I couldn't help that." An automaton, all wax and wires, hidden in the convincing guise of a demure customer service employee, but the linguist found the encounter disquieting, disorienting. Even so, she thinks the squeamishness we feel now needn't always constitute an obstacle. She can recall the period, in the seventies, when the first home-answering machines were similarly off-putting. Older folk in particular were frequently at a loss for words when confronted with the shock of the beep. "But there's nobody there," they complained to Baron, then a young researcher. The appropriate phrases, short, crisp, unruffled: the "Hi, it's grandma," and the "Just wanted to hear how your day went" and the "Can you give me a quick call when you get this?" all took time to acquire. But acquire them, in the end, they did.

I think it's fair to say that Baron is a techno-optimist. But she is quick to raise her own reservations. What if the naive, the vulnerable, are taken in by online talk sharks? By programmers without all their scruples, whose chatbots preach, browbeat, coquet? As Baron says this, tales of email scams — a heart broken here, a thousand dollars lost there — come to mind; if you think that a swindler's typed-out text can achieve so much, it is easy to imagine how much more persuasive a sweet-talking program might be. Indefatigable, unpunishable, they would roam freely along the Internet's electronic byways, ready at all hours to snare, to trick, to fleece their next victim.

"And what if a robot won't accept no for an answer?" Baron wonders. There is unease in her voice. She asks me to picture an old woman living in a nursing home. The home doesn't have enough caretakers to go around. To save time, the staff assigns the old woman a talking robot. The robot is strict: three times a day — morning, noon, and night — it must see that its patient takes her tablets. But say the old woman is headstrong. She wasn't always sick and old. Say she was once a bigwig, her career filled with clash and ego, and now cannot stand to take orders from a jumped-up cash register. "Ms. Henderson, it's time for your medication." The robot repeats itself when the old woman pretends not to hear. "Ms. Henderson, you must take your medication," it intones. "Your pulse is currently five beats below the normal level." It utters something about blood sugars too, but the old woman still doesn't budge. With her child—assuming she had a child—she might relent and throw the little blue pill into her mouth; with a nurse—after a respectable amount of fuss—she would finally sluice it down with a large tumbler of water. But with a robot? Never!

"If the old woman is still sprightly, if her faculties are still intact, then she can always go for the off switch, I suppose. That's the big difference between robots and humans: having an off switch," Baron says. What, though, she worries aloud, if the rules of human-robot conduct prevent this, forbid patients to unplug their caregiver? Robots talking patients into obedience on one side, and, on the other, patients unwilling to hear the machine out: textbook conditions for a shouting match. "When you overhear a row between neighbors in an apartment block, or between a customer and a member of staff in a shop, that's unpleasant enough as it is. How then would we react to a war of words in which one of the protagonists is mechanical?"

A program that sweet-talked or squabbled persuasively would have a good chance of disproving Descartes. Three hundred years before the digital computer was invented, he wrote this in his *Discourse on Method and Meditations on First Philosophy*:

If there were machines which bore a resemblance to our bodies and imitated our actions as closely as pos-

sible for all practical purposes, we should still have ...
very certain means of recognizing that they were not
real men ... they could never use words, or put
together signs, as we do in order to declare our
thoughts to others. For we can certainly conceive of a
machine so constructed that it utters words, and even
utters words that correspond to bodily actions causing
a change in its organs (for example, if one touches it
in some spot, the machine asks what it is that one
wants to say to it; if in another spot, it cries that one
has hurt it, and so on), but it is inconceivable that
such a machine should produce different arrange-
ments of words so as to give an appropriately meaningful answer to whatever is said in its presence, as
the dullest of men can do.

Descartes' language test was a thought experiment, a
seventeenth-century defense of the specialness of human
reasoning; it wasn't intended to be operational. But the Turing test (named for the British pioneer of computer science,
Alan Turing), first advanced in 1950, proposes a simple
means of putting through its paces a program's ability to
talk.

It goes like this. An "interrogator" sits alone in a room
before a computer screen. He is wielding a keyboard, and
the messages he sends in quick succession go out to a pair of
respondents in separate rooms. One is a man or woman who
replies to the interrogator's questions and comments as any
man or woman might. The other is a program, built to

interact just like a confirmed talker. The interrogator has five minutes to tell the two apart. Puns, jokes, idiosyncratic turns of conversation: all forms of talk are permitted. If, after the dialogues, the two remain indistinguishable, the program passes, and we can discard Descartes' objection: a machine will be said to have conversed.

Yet Eliza, Evie, and the other chatbots remain very far indeed from passing. So far, in fact, that you wonder whether Descartes' *inconceivable* means not only unthinkable—as a flying machine might once have been unthinkable—but also impossible: impossible as a pig that flies. Talk as somehow fundamentally robot-proof. The clumsy exclamations, the non sequiturs, the wisecracks that time and again fall flat as card castles: the computer's failure to say the right things does indeed seem telling. Its prowess in other disciplines, improving by leaps and bounds, makes the failure all the more remarkable. Programs have for years outperformed even the strongest chess masters and played checkers to perfection— literally. At the time of this writing, a program has for the first time bested a human champion at the ancient strategic game of go. (The human in question, a twenty-three-year-old South Korean, boasted in a prematch press conference that he would wallop the machine five to nothing; he lost four to one.) And then there are the face-recognizing programs, the knee-bending robots, the quiz-show-question–answering machines. Only the computer's language smarts still leave much to be desired. Only in the area of language is a Cartesian disdain toward the machine still tenable. The computer stands tongue-tied; and its silence grows newsworthier by the year.

It isn't for any want of trying. For twenty-five years, an American businessman has reportedly offered $100,000 to the designer of the first chatbot crafty enough to fool a majority of its human interrogators. Every year programmers enter their latest creations — complete with first names, family names, and biographies — into the competition; and, in fairness to the programmers, every now and then one of the more gullible or unimaginative judges mistakes a bot's "quirkiness" for a foreign adolescent's snark. That is the exception, though. The most fluent, thoughtful, engaging texts, the programs never manufacture. They never "produce different arrangements of words so as to give an appropriately meaningful answer to whatever is said in its presence, as the dullest of men can do." Not once has the businessman been at any risk of being separated from his money. And the annual publicity the media gives his contest certainly does his business no harm.

Some days after my discussion with the linguist, it occurs to me that I might need the advice of someone who spends time with these programs. Someone who knows bytes from RAMs. I don't have that kind of knowledge. A computer's innards are a total mystery to me. I talk it over with a friend, an information technologist. He goes quiet. Then he tells me not to delve into the technical side of things, that it isn't necessary, and he suggests a name: Harry Collins. Not a computer specialist as such, it turns out, but a sociologist doing interesting work on the Turing test.

I email Collins and make an appointment to call his office at the University of Cardiff. He sounds like a man between meetings when I telephone. For an instant, I dread having to tell my friend that the discussion with his sociologist came to nothing; but, very quickly, my anxieties evaporate. Collins's tight schedule (in the course of our conversation he mentions having three academic textbooks in the works) has made him curt, but also focused. He explains everything briskly and precisely, and I feel grateful for that succinct precision: a question saver.

On the present chatbots and their makers:

"The businessman's contest is nonsense. It's only a measure of *doing best* rather than of actually *doing*. But even the least worst bot can't talk. It can't converse. It can't use human language appropriately. Some of those in the field — the most optimistic — say, 'Wait another twenty years. You'll see.' Frankly, I don't believe them. They're hypesters; they'll say anything."

On the Turing test:

I've performed my own experiments that are variations on the Turing test. The same setup: the computer screens and the keyboards and the separate rooms and so on, but with a second person on the receiving end rather than a program. Human to human, as in real life. The idea is to better understand how we humans communicate, how we make ourselves understood, how we employ language to pass for one of us and for a particular kind of person.

In one experiment, we had a group of colorblind subjects. We said to them, "Reply to the interrogator's messages as though you can see colors just fine. So, for example, if an interrogator asks for your favorite color, you type back, *blue* or *yellow* or *fire-engine red,* you name it, even though you've never seen anything blue or yellow or red in your life. The idea was to explore how they performed in the language of those who see the world in color.

Collins reports that his subjects performed flawlessly. Without difficulty they discussed flower arranging, spun tales about playing snooker, described their impatience at waiting in their car for a traffic light to turn to green. Their interrogators couldn't tell whether they truly saw colors or not. The reason, he explains, is that the subjects had all been immersed from birth in a color-seers' society; in it, they had acquired the language down even to familiar expressions about "seeing red" or "feeling blue."

Collins took Turing's imitation game a stage further in a second experiment. He asked a group of blind subjects to converse at distance with their seeing interrogators. The subjects used screen-reader software to hear the keys pressed and the words formed as they typed their answers. "They had all lost their sight when very small, by the age of two or three, so they had no memory of the visual world." Even so, the interrogators were unable to determine from what their correspondents wrote that they were blind. The visually impaired, raised in a society in which vision pre-dominates, had "sighted language." To every question they could provide a "right type of answer."

I ask Collins for an example of the questions posed to these subjects. "Well, for instance: 'Around how many millimeters must a tennis ball drop from the line to be considered out?'"

They had never held a racket or swiveled their head left and right, left and right, to follow a tennis match. But they knew family or friends who had. And some of them had listened to sports commentaries on the radio.

"Then we turned things around. We asked a group of seeing subjects to type-talk as though they couldn't see and had no memory of having ever seen. In a word, to use 'blind language.'" They couldn't. The interrogators, who were all blind, were able to tell right from the opening question that the subjects were only pretending."

The interrogators' first question was the simple-seeming "How old were you when you went blind?"

Collins: "The subjects would say things like 'two years old' or 'I lost my sight when I was three,' whereas a blind person will reply something like 'It began when I was two, and I was registered blind at three and a half.'"

Because they hadn't been raised by blind parents or mixed with blind friends, the seeing subjects had never learned how the nonseeing speak among themselves. They had never learned that to speak of going blind was to speak of a gradual process.

"What the subjects in these tests, the colorblind and the blind, were doing wasn't guesswork. They weren't attempting to 'talk the talk.' Something else, something far more interesting, was going on. The subjects displayed a sort of language know-how. They knew what *green* or *tennis* meant, but more importantly they knew precisely how talkers in green-seeing and tennis-playing societies use these words in everyday conversation. They could reproduce the appropriate conversational behavior at any given moment. They could 'walk the talk.'"

Language as a stand-in for the body, as a substitute for direct experience: conversational Human is the outcome of our "talk walking." Often that talk is small. But, Collins adds, there are occasions when it has to turn more complicated, when we must address a lawyer, for example, or a doctor, and conversation suddenly comes less easily. Even so, most defendants and patients manage. An average person's language know-how can be surprisingly broad and deep.

To test just how deep, in 2006 Collins performed his most impressive experiment. On himself. "I'm a sociologist of scientific knowledge. I've spent my career studying the men and women who do gravitational wave physics. I've hung out with them. Talked for hours on end with them. Immersed myself in their community. Now, I can't perform any of their calculations, no one would ever let me loose on a soldering iron, but I can talk just as they talk. So one day I decided to put my money where my mouth was."

Collins asked a panel of gravitational wave physicists to send him and a gravitational wave physicist a list of questions to answer separately. One of the questions went as follows:

A theorist tells you that she has come up with a theory in which a circular ring of particles is displaced by gravitational waves so that the circular shape remains the same but the size oscillates about a mean size. Would it be possible to measure this effect using a laser interferometer?

The physicist wrote back:

Yes, but you should analyze the sum of the strains in the two arms, rather than the difference. In fact, you don't even need two arms of an interferometer to detect gravitational waves, provided you can measure the roundtrip light travel time along a single arm accurately enough to detect small changes in its length.

Collins, simulating a physicist, replied:

It depends on the direction of the source. There will be no detectable signal if the source lies anywhere on the plane that passes through the centre station and bisects the angle of the two arms. Otherwise there will be a signal, maximized when the source lies along one or other of the two arms.

Out of the nine judges on the panel, seven considered the quality of the answers to their questions to be identical. Only two dared to identify the nonphysicist. Neither chose Collins.

"Apparently, in one of his responses the genuine physicist had drawn on ideas from a published paper. I hadn't come across that paper. I had to come up with my own answer. The two judges thought, 'Only a genuine physicist could write something like this.'"

Collins passed this version of the Turing test because, like his colorblind and blind subjects, he had gained enough "interactional expertise."

"Reading papers and books and newspapers alone won't do. You have to spend time, lots of time, in conversation with people who know from experience what they are talking about."

I agree with Collins. I tell him his theory matches my experience as a writer. In preparation for my novel *Mishenka,* the story of a Soviet chess grandmaster's intuitive search for meaning, I spoke in person and at length with several grandmasters. I visited the home of the former world champion Vladimir Kramnik, the feller of Garry Kasparov, and drew anecdote after anecdote out of him. In Paris I sat backstage amid the analysts and reporters at a tournament in which the world's strongest players were competing. All in order to put myself in my character's thoughts.

"Exactly. *You* can do that, whereas no one can think up a way computers might ever socialize. They haven't a body. Maybe they don't require a lot of body. Maybe a tongue and larynx, a pair of ears and eyes, the mechanical equivalents, would be sufficient. But then, how do we go about embedding the machine in a human speech community? Making it a participant in the circulation of meanings? The very notion seems to me to be a nonstarter."

A nonstarter. Why then did Turing foresee fluent machines

in the course of the twentieth century? (He wrote that machines would likely converse with ease by the year 2000.) Probably, with his head for data, he assumed that conversation could eventually be boiled down to a science. Many other intellectuals of the postwar period believed that the brain was a squishy computer, that human language was nothing more than a digital code. The metaphor, even its critics admit, has the benefit of being seductive. Clingy. Through the disappointment of failed predictions, its popularity has survived.

"I blame Chomsky," Mark Bickhard says. Bickhard, a philosopher of language, is speaking to me from his home in Pennsylvania via Skype. He says,

Back in the fifties, his work was all the rage, and of course it still has clout. Essentially, Chomsky claims that you and I understand sentences because of their structure—the order of the words, rules of grammar, and so on. I have two things to say about that. One, yes, of course language is in part structural, but then so too are any number of skills. Fire-making, for example, has its own syntax: you have to perform all the different subtasks—collecting the tinder and kindling, striking a match, blowing onto the logs—in a particular order for the fire to burn. That doesn't make fire-making a language. Two, learning theory has come a long way since the fifties; we now know the huge role played by situational context, and the many intricate semantic relationships between words, in how we communicate.

*　　*　　*

Bickhard is seventy, with a bald dome and intense eyes. As befits a resident of Bethlehem (Pennsylvania), he has a prophet's long white whiskers. Behind his desk, on a side table, sit thick books atop even thicker books. He came to language by accident, he tells me. Forty years ago, after writing a dissertation on psychotherapy, he was told it contained too much math and was asked to include a chapter on language. Bickhard spent "a whole bunch of years" studying and rejecting every linguistic model then available. But his fascination with what makes language language remained.

Language, according to Bickhard, is dynamic. Like Rorschach blots, words need to be constantly interpreted, and always require us to do some filling in. "You walk down some old wooden stairs, and one of the steps creaks. Instantly, you know what that creak means: 'Gee, I'd better get off—it's about to break.' Well, the same sort of thing happens all the time with words. A father who hears his little boy say something like 'I buttoned the calculator' understands him perfectly, knows exactly how to respond to him, even if, strictly speaking, the words themselves are nonsense.

"Or, imagine you hear someone shout, 'Roast beef at table three needs water.' Nonsense, too. Unless, that is, you're sitting in a restaurant. Waiter talk."

In any given situation, the meaning of a word, a phrase, unfolds dynamically. It cannot be second-guessed. "You're in a restaurant. You take a menu and you order. 'Roast beef,' you say. The waiter returns a while later with your dish." For

Bickhard, there is always much more going on than meets the ear. "What we have to ask ourselves is this: how does uttering 'roast beef' change the social reality in which the speaker participates?"

Does uttering *roast beef* carry a higher social value than, say, *pork chop?* Does the waiter, who took you for a vegetarian, see you henceforth with different eyes? Does the utterer's friend at the same table conceal a grin as his memory sings "This little piggy had roast beef, this little piggy had none"?

"Words transform the world around us. Learning a language is learning how *roast beef* transforms a situation compared to *roast chicken* or indeed *I'm tired, the one over there,* or *See you around.*"

I'm listening carefully to Bickhard, my pen running fast with notes, when all of a sudden our connection gives out: the philosopher vanishes in mid-sentence. Minutes pass. Finally, he calls me back and the screen fills again with his white beard and navy-blue sweater and the side-table pile of books.

Humans in conversation, he concludes, update and modify social reality from moment to moment. Meanings are broached, negotiated, tussled over. Big things are at stake. Computers, on the other hand, inert and indifferent, "can't care less" about meaning. It is this can't-care-less-ness that will forever keep them imitating people's words.

I care about the philosopher's words. They can change me, and I let them. When I turn off my laptop it feels warm. I notice that. Not the warm of a friend's hug or handshake; only of electricity, I think. But without it, how much less of the world's meaning would our brains transform, convert?

ACKNOWLEDGMENTS

I am grateful to my first reader, Jérôme Tabet, and to our respective families — in particular, my mother, Jennifer, my siblings, and Catherine Tabet, Nicole Thibault, Raymonde Tabet, and Patrick Tabet — for their abiding encouragement. Also to my friends Ian and Ana Williams, Oliver and Ash Jeffery, Sigriður Kristinsdóttir and Hallgrímur Helgi Helgason, Valgerður Benediktsdóttir and Grímur Björnsson, Laufey Bjarnadóttir and Torfi Magnússon, Linda Flah, Claire Bertrand and her family, Valérie Leclerc and Arnaud Salembier, Jérémie Giles, Helen and Rick Zipes, Aurélia Chapelain and Didier Delgado, Agnès and Nicolas Ciaravola, Emilie and Jérôme Jude, Sonia Velli, Caroline Ravel, Yoann Milin and Marianne Cruciani, Guy and Nadine Landais, Martin Johnson and Kristina, and Leandro Jofré for the many hours of stimulating and multilingual conversation.

The essay "Talking Hands" would never have been possible without the hospitality and unstinting support of Margo Flah and Jean-Philippe Tabet. Immense thanks to Monica Elaine Campbell and Michel David.

For their precious contributions to this book, my gratitude also goes to Erin McKean; Les Murray and Margaret Connolly; Eszter Besenyei, Peter Weide, Ulrich Lins, Renato

Corsetti, Ken Miner, and W. H. Jansen; Ngũgĩ wa Thiong'o, Wangui wa Goro, Gichingiri Ndigirigi, and Evan Mwangi; Richard Ringler; Brian Stowell, Adrian Cain, and Paul Weatherall of Manx National Heritage; Sir Michael Edwards; David Bellos and Gilles Esposito-Farese; Erri De Luca and Andy Minch; Wayne A. Beach and Lana Rakow; and Naomi Susan Baron, Harry Collins, and Mark Bickhard.

Thank you to my English and American editors, Rowena Webb and Tracy Behar, and to their diligent teams, particularly Ian Straus, Pamela Marshall, and Kathryn Rogers — and also to Andrew Lownie, my agent.

ABOUT THE AUTHOR

Daniel Tammet is an essayist, novelist, and translator. He is the author of *Thinking in Numbers*, *Embracing the Wide Sky*, and the *New York Times* bestseller *Born on a Blue Day*. Tammet is a Fellow of the Royal Society of Arts (FRSA). He lives in Paris.